Peril in Panama

China as the Gatekeeper of the Panama Canal Threatens new Missile Crisis

By Richard A. Delgaudio
President, National Security Center

Introduction by Captain G. Russell Evans, USCG (Ret.)

published by
National Security Center
P.O. Box 96571
Washington, DC 20090-6571

November 1, 1998

this book is dedicated to:

my children:
Kara Louise Delgaudio,
Jason Alexander Delgaudio, and
Army-Ranger (in-training at this publication date)
Richard Lee Delgaudio.

and to the

Retired Military Officers Advisory Board
of National Security Center
They have laid aside their uniform,
but not their love of country.

Also published by National Security Center

Death Knell of the Panama Canal?
by Captain G. Russell Evans, USCG (Ret.), Introduction by
Admiral Thomas Moorer, USN (Ret.).

Red Star Over the Panama Canal
(A Report on the 1998 Mission to Panama)
By Richard A. Delgaudio

Big Trouble in Panama
(1998 Testimony before U.S. Senate Foreign Relations
Committee) By Admiral Thomas Moorer, USN (Ret.)

Cover design/art by Paul D'Innocenzo, New York, N.Y.
Special Thanks to the Chairman of the Board of National Security Center, Don Derham

ISBN 0-9658348-1-6
98-067470

Acknowledgements

I don't work alone. This book was made possible by some great teamwork. This section is about that team.

A major contributor to this work won't let me name him. I used to be in his line of work (for over ten years), raising funds for Reagan for President, Helms for Senate and other conservative causes and candidates. I appreciate what he does for me, National Security Center and our cause.

Captain G. Russell Evans, USCG (Ret.), author of the first book published by National Security Center, *Death Knell of the Panama Canal?* is chief advisor to NSC on the Panama Canal. Captain Evans is a constant source of inspiration and information on this important issue and has been associated with NSC for nearly ten years. He is the editor of *Panama Alert* newsletter, published by NSC, and has participated in the first three "Mission to Panama" fact finding trips. His wife's constant support proves the adage, behind every great man is a great woman.

The Retired Military Officers Advisory Board of National Security Center, especially its Honorary Chairman, Admiral Thomas Moorer, USN (Ret.), former Chairman of the Joint Chiefs of Staff, who wrote the introduction to our book, *Death Knell of the Panama Canal?* and who recently testified about our concerns before Senator Jesse Helms' Foreign Relations Committee of the U.S. Senate.

Dan Lewis, NSC research chief on our Mission to Panama, for *Death Knell of the Panama Canal?*, and for this book. Dan was the director of the videotaping for all interviews on the recent Mission to Panama trip and the forthcoming video documentary, *Checkmate, China Controls the Canal.* He has also done fundraising and writing work for Buchanan for President and Helms for U.S. Senate.

James Florez of Virginia performed translator duties and was Chief Videographer on the Mission to Panama trip.

Several supporters of National Security Center paid their own way (and part of ours) to participate in this Mission to Panama trip, including: Bob Scholl of Arden, NC, Ammon C. Adams of Oregon, and Winchell T. Hayward of California, who also asked some very penetrating questions in the interviews and on several occasions served as our backup photographer and videographer.

We have good friends in Panama who love their country every bit as much as we love ours. Their help in research for this book and in opening doors for interviews is deeply appreciated. They include: Ray Bishop, formerly the head of a major labor union in Panama serving the workers on military bases, has recently organized the largest association in Panama to unite all those who work to maintain and operate U.S. military bases and installations as well as the Canal itself. Bishop was the main organizer on our most recent trip in Panama and led a 5-person Panamanian delegation to the USA to meet with U.S. Senators, Congressmen and staff to brief them on the situation in Panama in transition.

William Bright Marine, a citizen of both the U.S.A. and Panama, whose research information has been invaluable, and who shared his information at our meetings in Panama.

Other Panamanians who helped our "Mission to Panama": Ms. Eulalia (Laly) Lane, Mr. Luis "Famoso" Rivera, Mr. William Lopez (the latter all came to Washington in September, 1998), Mr. Alberto Torres, Mr. Andy Aleman, Mr. Leonardo Hunt, Mr. Ernesto Bennett, Mr. Rujilio Thinwall.

And finally, a special thank you to these unsung heroes whose help has been invaluable for our cause.

1. Our supporters whose donations made this all possible and whose future support keep the wind beneath our wings.

2. The many people I met with personally in Panama who gave their expertise and opinion but who cannot be named for fear of retribution. This includes military officers, (retired and active); both American and Panamanian nationals who work on the Canal itself, and others. Their giving of their time and their expertise is deeply appreciated. Although I have not been able to attribute some of the information and views directly to you (as you requested) I appreciate your insight and information.

3. The people of Panama who by 3 to 1 margin, want the U.S. to continue helping operate and keep safe, their national treasure and our common national heritage, the Panama Canal. A special thank you to those Panamanians whose good work helped operate and safeguard the Canal for all these years. Firing 3,800 of you during the past year that U.S. installations have been turned over to the government of Panama, is a lousy way of saying "thank you for a job well done." We hope the future is better, and it will be, if there is change in the current policy of both our countries.

4. Those Americans who have reached out a hand of friendship to Panama, and signed the "Solidarity" Statement of support for our pro-USA, anti-Red China friends in Panama. This includes Representatives Philip Crane, Dan Burton, Bob Barr and Barbara Cubin. Prominent conservatives who signed this Solidarity Statement are U.S. Presidential Candidate and friend, Gary Bauer, Former Chairman of the Joint Chiefs of Staff Admiral Thomas Moorer (USN, Ret.), Admiral James Carey (USN, Ret.- President of Conservative Network), Grover Norquist (President of Americans for Tax Reform), noted author, TV commentator and columnist, Phyllis Schlafly, James Martin (President of 60 Plus), Captain G. Russell Evans.

5. Kathy Wimmer, our full-charge bookkeeper and office manager and all of our behind-the-scenes suppliers. Your professionalism and dedication is deeply appreciated.

6. My Mom, also the world's greatest Grandmother.

INTRODUCTION

By Captain G. Russell Evans, USCG (Ret.)

Some people never give up — especially when they know they are right. Chief among these are Richard A. Delgaudio of the National Security Center (NSC) and our friend, Admiral Tom Moorer, former Chairman of the Joint Chiefs of Staff, a top military strategist and the Honorary Chairman of National Security Center's Retired Military Officers Advisory Board.

Now Richard's new book, *Peril in Panama*, provides an important update on Red China's quiet takeover of the strategic ports of the Panama Canal and the sneaky Panama Law No. 5 that runs roughshod over U.S. rights guaranteed by the 1977 Carter-Torrijos Panama Canal Treaties. Meanwhile, our media seems completely preoccupied with the ongoing and endless Clinton/Gore scandals. Congress appears too busy to demand an accounting of the President for his policy regarding America's national security and national honor at the Isthmus of Panama.

Law No. 5, passed under secretive conditions and without any consultations with old friend, the United States, blatantly violates the Panama Canal Treaties: Art. V of the Neutrality Treaty by leasing defense sites to Hutchison Port Holdings, an ally of Communist China, when Panama *only* is allowed in defense sites; Art. VI guarantees "expeditious passage" and "head of line" to U.S. warships, but Law No. 5 gives Hutchison "priority operations". Even Panama's Constitution was violated in Art. 274 which requires a plebiscite for Canal matters. None was held. In the rush to turn the Canal into a short-term cash cow, greed was the creed.

In official documents, the United States is "China's main enemy". Sec. IV of the Communist Manifesto calls for the "forcible overthrow" of the capitalist system. Now, with Law No. 5, Red China can operate submarines and other warships from former U.S. defense sites, as well as attack bombers. Ballistic missiles, now perfected with U.S. technology thanks to a Clinton/Gore waiver that looks like a *quid pro quo*, can be launched from these defense sites 900 miles from America.

Canal workers are being fired in droves — some 3800 recently — in shameless violations of the spirit and intent of Art. X of the 1977 Panama Canal Treaties. Panamanian labor leader Ray Bishop, called the Lech Walesa of Panama, has courageously defended rights of the workers, much as the famous Polish leader did in the 1980's against another oppressive regime.

The findings of the Delgaudio-led 1998 Mission to Panama were very similar to those of five previous missions — perhaps more so, if possible — and last minute cancellations by high-ranking officials commonplace when the truth would hurt. Nonetheless, this book reports alarming, new developments — chief of which is the very real threat to the Canal with Red China set to seize it after the Americans quietly depart at noon, December 31st, 1999 — a scant year away.

If the Washington Administration and the Congress had the courage, the unconstitutional 1977 Panama

Treaties could be terminated because of "changing circumstances" as authorized by Art. 62 of the Vienna Convention on the Law of Treaties 1969. But, who has the courage when complacence will do? And who cares about Tom Paine, Revolutionary War hero, who wrote, "It is an affront to treat falsehood with complacence".

In a previous NSC book, *Death Knell of the Panama Canal?*, the six "notes" of the death knell are carefully explained:

- Red China as "gatekeeper" at each end of the Canal.

- Panama Law No. 5 with far-reaching "rights" to Hutchison, ally of Red China, violating the Panama Treaties and U.S. rights in a 50-year lease.

- Cousins and cronies of Panama's President Balladares to run the Canal.

- Canal worn-out from "neglect and lack of maintenance" reported in the Army Corps of Engineers Study.

- The continuing unconstitutional Panama Treaties, conflict in defense rights between DeConcini Condition and Panama's counter-reservation, now with Red China in the middle.

- Abject failure of our media to report these dangers and criminal neglect of Clinton/Gore to challenge and correct them.

Some editors whine that the Canal issue was "settled 20 years ago". It certainly was not, and only the courage and persistence of organizations like the

National Security Center can save the day. Personally, I'm very proud to have been an NSC advisor for ten years and to see the dedication — often against great odds.

Readers of this courageous new book, and supporters of the National Security Center, are well-informed — though probably in the minority since too many know-it-all columnists and commentators have pooh-poohed the danger to the U.S.A. at the Canal.

Indeed, it is our duty to notify the Oval Office and stalwarts in the halls of Congress, in very strong terms, that we want action and 1) that Hutchison Port Holdings, ally of Red China, or any other Communist-affiliated entity, is unacceptable as "gatekeeper" of the Panama Canal, 2) that Panama Law No. 5 is unacceptable because of blatant violations of the 1977 Panama Canal Treaties and 3) that the Panama Canal Treaties themselves must be abrogated because of "changing circumstances" under Art. 62 of the Vienna Convention on the Law of Treaties 1969.

When the Washington authorities, sworn to defend our country, send back an aide-dispatched form letter totally unresponsive, patience and more patience is required to get answers for, after all, "Action can only come from ourselves . . . our only strength, our only security, lies in the individual" (Calvin Coolidge).

Norfolk, Virginia   G. Russell Evans
November 1, 1998   Captain, USCG (Ret.)

Chief Project Advisor to
National Security Center on the Panama Canal

PREFACE

As President of National Security Center, a Washington area national defense think tank and action group, I sift through a lot of information that reaches me from a variety of sources. One confidential source told me in early 1997 that a corporation allied with Red China, had just secured far-reaching "rights" and control over several key installations at the Panama Canal — including the Canal entrance/exit ports of Balboa on the Pacific Ocean side, and Cristobal on the Atlantic Ocean side. Red China in the Western Hemisphere? It certainly sounded far-fetched to me. If this information were really true, then it would make Red China the new "Gatekeeper" of the Panama Canal.

If Red China had quietly moved in to become the new Gatekeeper of the most "vital waterway in the world" as former Chairman of the Joint Chiefs of Staff, Admiral Thomas Moorer, has described the Panama Canal, the implications for future U.S. national security interests would be disastrous.

It would be a full year of intense research and investigation before our NSC analysts and I would develop an even more disastrous national security scenario. That is: Red China's intermediate nuclear missiles transferred to Panama via container ships and quietly offloaded. The dream of the Soviet Union from 1962, to put the less expensive, more accurate, shorter-range nuclear missiles right in America's back yard, realized by another communist super-power, Red China.

I shared this information about Red China at the Panama Canal with Captain G. Russell Evans, the eminent authority on Panama Canal matters who has been our chief project advisor for a decade. We gathered additional documentary information.

This stunning news about Red China's emergence as a power on the American continent–a massive reversal of the many-decades old Monroe Doctrine, had not been reported in any U.S. media. With rare exception, today, over a year later, it still hasn't.

We continued to report new facts confirming Red China's emergence as "Gatekeeper" of the Panama Canal in our publications, including briefing reports, several issues of *Panama Alert* newsletter and a briefing at the 1997 and 1998 Conservative Political Action Conferences.

Today, one year later, there has still been very little information about Red China at the Panama Canal reported in U.S. news media.

This book is the product of many hundreds of hours of research by the National Security Center research and analysis team over the past year, including my recent trip to Panama with several key team members to investigate this infiltration of the Panama Canal by Red China. What we discovered in this "Mission to Panama" confirms our worst suspicions. Red China has in fact emerged as the "Gatekeeper" of the Panama Canal.

Red China is the greatest threat to American security in the world. It has openly declared the U.S. as its primary enemy in the world. Red China is focused on winning a war with America. It has the largest army in the world and is rapidly building up its navy and air force. In fact, Red China is increasing its military spending faster than any other country in the world — including the United States. Until recently, Red China was the only country in the world which still targeted its nuclear missiles at American cities. The announcement of a change in this policy by President Clinton is as dubious as some of his other claims, because the re-targeting can be done in a matter of minutes. Seventy percent of Red China's inter-continental ballistic nuclear missiles were aimed at the U.S. Recently, U.S. intelligence discovered that another half dozen ICBM's had been deployed by Red China and that tests of these missiles had continued even while President Clinton was on Chinese soil boasting of his friendship with Red China's leaders.

In March of 1997 Hutchison Whampoa — a Hong Kong based business whose owner is a close ally of Red China — took over operation of key ports at the Panama Canal. These ports were turned over to Hutchison Whampoa even though American and other companies submitted better bids. This contract gave Hutchison Whampoa certain "rights" that could eventually give them and their Red Chinese ally complete control over the Panama Canal when the U.S. completes its phased withdrawal in 1999.

National Security Center began sounding the alarm about this infiltration of the Panama Canal as soon as we heard about the Hutchison Whampoa deal. Some in Congress were alarmed at our news. But others naively dismissed the threat posed by Red China and the infiltration of the Canal by Hutchison Whampoa.

That is why I have written this book. Because the takeover of the Panama Canal by Red China is a serious security threat to the United States. There is a clear and direct threat to, not just the security of the nation of Panama and the Canal, but the security of the United States itself. This book will detail the national security threat posed by the takeover of the Panama Canal by an ally of Red China. It will show conclusively how closely Hutchison Whampoa and its head, Li Ka-shing, are tied to Red China. It will show how Hutchison Whampoa and Red China have maneuvered into the Panama Canal ports and how they are poised to take over other critical installations. And finally this book will explain how the takeover of the Panama Canal military installations will enable China to target a whole new class of nuclear missiles at the United States — leading to a new missile crisis where a hundred American cities and the lives of millions of Americans could be erased by the push of a button controlled by Red China's brutal communist leaders.

All the evidence indicates that Red China's intentions are to fight and win a future military confrontation with the United States. As you will see in this book, some of our most credible experts believe Red China will win such a future confrontation. Yet our leaders have remained silent while Red China has moved to take over the strategic Panama Canal ports.

Two separate questions. First, why has our President allowed this development? Second, why did key "leaders" of the opposition party remain silent while this happened (and why do they remain silent today)?

The easier question first. Red China has been documented as a major campaign contributor for Bill Clinton's reelection campaign. It is beyond the purview of this book to document and prove the exact quid pro quo arrangements which took place. Let me just say that I believe Red China has got its money's worth from those campaign contributions to Bill Clinton.

The second question has a less than obvious answer. And that is, today as in 1976 when Ronald Reagan ran for President, the power-elite of both political parties just don't want to talk about the Panama Canal topic. Either because they favor the new arrangements, are fearful of being held to account by their constituents, or they are simply ignorant of the importance of this issue to our country. Surprisingly, I find that many otherwise reasonable conservative leaders believe that their ignorance on this issue confirms the non-importance of this issue. Quite a paradox. I call it "confirmed ignorance."

The American people and our elected officials in Washington, D.C. will learn the truth if they read this book: the United States faces a serious national security crisis - and a new missile crisis in the future- from this takeover of the Panama Canal by Red China.

I. RED CHINA: ENEMY #1

Red China has emerged as the premier strategic and military threat to U.S. security in the world. It has the largest population (more than four times the population of the U.S.) in the world. This massive population allows Red China to put 3 million men on active duty and 12 million more in the reserves — the world's largest military force. The army (the largest in the world) has 2,290,000 men under arms. The navy has 240,000 members, including about 25,000 in the naval air force and another 6,000 in the marines. These naval personnel operate as many as 1700 vessels, including more than 90 submarines, one of them armed with nuclear missiles. The air force has 470,000 members, including 220,000 in air defense. They fly an estimated 5000 combat aircraft. Red China has 18 intercontinental nuclear missiles, 13 of which were pointed at American cities, and over 100 intermediate and medium range nuclear missiles.

At this writing, what the American media call the "modernization" of Red China's nuclear missile forces has just added another six long range nuclear missiles to this force. Reports abound about the latest U.S. technology being made available to Red China, to enable those missiles to strike at American targets more accurately than ever before. An even more modern factory complex is being finalized at this writing, to enable a faster and larger "modernization" program in the future.

China is one of the last remaining communist countries. As such it is still bent on the destruction of capitalism, especially in the United States. And the government in Beijing is still a brutally repressive totalitarian regime, which stamps on the rights and liberties of its citizens and foreigners alike. Red China continues to jam the Voice of America, so that their people don't hear information contrary to their propaganda. They refuse to let the International Red Cross have access to their prisons, where most inmates are political prisoners. Political protesters in China are often arrested, and some even disappear — never to be heard from again. Even foreigners are subject to Red China's harsh rule. Anyone caught committing illegal political "activities" like distributing religious pamphlets, for example, are arrested and held for days without being permitted to speak to their embassy. If they're lucky, only their money and possessions are taken from them before they are expelled.

And yet — with all this evidence — the assertion that Red China is the premier military and strategic threat to the U.S. is not universally held. In fact, there is a strong, perhaps even dominant, school of thought in the United States which believes that Red China is one of America's premier strategic and economic partners in the world. Supporters of this school of thought believe it is in America's interest to continue the de facto alliance with China that the U.S. had in the 1970's and 1980's. They tend to be concerned more with economic issues (i.e. doing business in China) and dismiss China's military threats and human rights violations. One legislator in California confided in me that his speaking out on the Red China threat earned him a sharp rebuke from his party's leaders, anxious not to offend those businessmen who seek deals with China.

But the fact of the matter is that China is indeed the prime national security threat to the United States, economics and the de facto alliance notwithstanding. An analogous situation would be the U.S. relationship with the Soviet Union during the Second World War. During the war, the Soviets were our allies against Nazi Germany — the greater threat to both nations at the time. Because both the U.S. and the Soviets were fighting a common enemy, they put their conflicting interests aside for a time. But soon after the defeat of Germany, a U.S.-Soviet rivalry emerged when it became clear the strategic interests of each country were at odds, and the Cold War began.

The American relationship with China in the 1990's is very similar to that American relationship with the Soviet Union. From the early 1970's when President Nixon went to China to the early 1990's, Washington and Beijing had an informal alliance directed against the Soviet Union. Both China and America put their conflicting interests on the back burner to deal with the more serious and imminent threat posed by the Soviets. With the collapse of the Eastern Bloc in 1989-1990 and the disintegration of the Soviet Union in 1992, the strategic partnership between America and China became obsolete. And, as with the U.S. and Soviet Union in 1945, the conflicting strategic interests of each country, which were put on the back burner, came to the fore.

STRATEGIC INTEREST IN CONFLICT

So what are these strategic interests, and why are they in conflict? Quite simply, the United States is the dominant power in Asia and the world, and Red China wants to take America's place. The system of government in the United States is held as the ideal in the world. Red China wants their system of communism to be the ideal.

It is important that means and ends not be confused. As Red China builds up its economy, develops its technology, and modernizes its military, one would expect that Red China would seek to expand its sphere of influence in the world and eventually supplant the United States as the dominant power in Asia and the world.

But the military buildup is not the result of an expansion in the Red Chinese economy alone. Rather, the purpose of the buildup is to project Red Chinese power. And Red China's leaders are far more willing to use their military power to project power and accomplish their goals, than most Americans expect.

Richard Bernstein and Ross H. Munro note in their book, *"The Coming Conflict with China",* that:

> "Within a few years, China will be the largest economy in the world, and it is on its way to becoming a formidable military power as well, one whose strength and influence are already far greater than those of any other country in the vast Pacific region, except for the United States.

China is an unsatisfied and ambitious power whose goal is to dominate Asia... by being so much more powerful than they are that nothing will be allowed to happen in East Asia without China's at least tacit consent."

China's short term goal, to dominate Asia and the Pacific, is in direct conflict with America's century-long strategic policy of preventing a dominant power from emerging in Asia. From the late 1800's to the early 1900's America's "Open Door" policy regarding China was intended to prevent a European power from dominating East Asia. America's focus shifted to preventing Japan from ascending in Asia in the 1930's, and of course the U.S. fought Japan for supremacy in the Pacific in World War II. During the Cold War, the U.S. aimed to contain Soviet expansion in Asia, and fought wars in Korea and Vietnam to keep the communists out. Today, with the fall of the Soviet Union and the constitutional limits on Japan's military power, only Red China remains to contest America's power for dominance in Asia. And they are already far down the path of confrontation with America for control of Asia.

CHINA'S THIRD STEP POLICY

China has always had a specific, three step policy to begin asserting their power in Asia. The first step was the takeover of Hong Kong, a city on the Chinese mainland which was under British control for 158 years. The second step was the takeover of Macau, a Portuguese possession also on the mainland. Finally, with the historic Chinese mainland under their control, the final step is the takeover of Taiwan, what Red China considers their "rebel" province.

The takeover of Hong Kong, step number one in Red China's emergence as the major Asian power, has already occurred. At midnight, June 30, 1997, the British Colony was formally handed over to Red China, which promised to follow a "one country, two systems" policy allowing freedom and democracy to continue. But China's promise was broken almost immediately. They abolished the duly elected legislature of Hong Kong and put in place a legislature appointed by the Red Chinese. Reports of press censorship emerged. Red China forced several Hong Kong businesses to hand over their companies to Beijing's control for minimum compensation. The Hong Kong police were given new power to control the citizens of Hong Kong, including the right to ban demonstrations. Laws which guaranteed labor rights were suspended. And the election process in Hong Kong was altered to make sure the pro-Communist candidates would win. Bernstein and Munro quote an architect of the new system in *"The Coming Conflict with China"*:

"The design is not simply from the consideration of democratic ideals," said on Lau Siukai, one of the drafters of the new rules who, perhaps unwittingly, admitted the primacy of politics over law. "We have to consider ... how to maintain good relations between the mainland and Hong Kong."

The Red Chinese takeover of Hong Kong has been invaluable to the communists. They have gained one of the richest and most impressive economic centers in the world. They have also taken control of a massive deep-water port strategically placed in the South China Sea. And they have gained the international prestige commensurate with the acquisition of such a valuable prize.

Next on Red China's list is Macau, a small colony of Portugal on the Chinese coast. Macau is scheduled to revert to Red Chinese control in 1999. The takeover of Macau will not be the major economic and political event that the takeover of Hong Kong was, to be sure. But the handover of this Portuguese colony still has great significance. With Macau in Red Chinese hands, Beijing will control all of historical mainland China. And with historical mainland China under their thumb, the communist leadership will be free to set their sights on overseas territorial acquisitions — specifically, Taiwan.

Taiwan is an island province of China and, since the Communist takeover of the Chinese mainland in 1949, the seat of the government of the Republic of China. It is separated from the Chinese mainland by the Taiwan Strait, but Red China still claims Taiwan as one of its provinces.

On December 8, 1949, following occupation of the mainland by the Communists, the Nationalist government of China, led by General Chiang Kai-shek, established its headquarters on Taiwan. Red China was prevented from invading Taiwan by the United States Navy. In April 1951 the United States further announced that U.S. military personnel would be sent to Taiwan to assist in the training of Nationalist forces. For the remainder of the 1950s, despite sporadic hostilities between Taiwan and the mainland, the United

States Navy defended Taiwan from invasion by the Red Chinese. In 1954, the U.S. signed a mutual-defense treaty with Taiwan by which the United States essentially agreed to defend against a Red Chinese attack. Since then, Taiwan has remained an American ally and the source of greatest friction between Red China and the United States.

This friction came to a head in 1996 when the Red Chinese conducted military "exercises" off the coast of Taiwan, including raining down missiles only miles from the capital of Taiwan. These military exercises were a blatant attempt to influence Taiwan's elections to help get the hard-line anticommunist candidates out of office. In response, the United States sent two U.S. Navy aircraft carriers to the Strait of Taiwan to warn the Red Chinese off. Red China did finally stop their exercises, but not before threatening to destroy Los Angeles with nuclear weapons if America continued to stand by Free China on Taiwan.

This event, the largest military face-off in the Pacific since World War II, could be an ominous sign of things to come. America must continue to support Free China on Taiwan or else lose international credibility and possibly shatter the entire U.S. alliance structure in the Pacific. But Red China has repeatedly asserted its intent to take over Taiwan — either peacefully or by force — American security guarantee or not.

Red China wants Taiwan because, of course, they want to re-conquer what they consider to be a rebel province. But Taiwan would also help Red China become the dominant naval power in East Asia in the

21st century. Taiwan sits astride the major strategic sea lanes in East Asia. Most of the commerce going to American allies like Japan and South Korea pass through these sea lanes. The naval and air bases in Taiwan would give Red China the ability to control these strategic sea lanes.

RED CHINA'S MILITARY BUILDUP

Red China's three step policy of taking over Hong Kong, Macau, and Taiwan would put Beijing in a very powerful strategic position. This improved strategic position would help Red China project its growing military power even more, and would facilitate their plan to dominate Asia.

The 2,290,000 man Peoples Liberation Army (PLA) is the dominant branch of the Red Chinese military. They have over 9000 tanks and 14,500 artillery pieces. The PLA is being rapidly reformed to fight effectively in modern battles, stressing flexibility and technological proficiency. Most military regions are building rapid reaction forces of highly mobile and fully equipped units to respond to a crisis or lead an invasion. And the PLA is making a concerted effort to improve their combined arms operations (an attack using the army, navy, and air force all at once to bring maximum firepower to bear) — a prerequisite for an attack on Taiwan or a conflict with the United States.

The impressive stature of the Red Chinese army was in the past mitigated by their weak navy and obsolete air force and a limited ability to project power (i.e. attack) overseas. But the programs to modernize the massive Red Chinese air force and the development of a "blue water" navy has opened the door for China's army throughout the Pacific rim.

Red China's aircraft development program has been the most active in the world in the 1990's. The Red Chinese air force consists of an estimated 5000 planes, many of which are modern attack aircraft based on high quality fighter/bomber Soviet designs.

The most important Red Chinese fighter aircraft is the J-11, a variant of the highly acclaimed Soviet Su-27. These modern attack aircraft have a range of over 1000 miles (depending on refueling) and can drop over 13,000 pounds of bombs on a single run. They can be used to attack targets on land or sea. China will have over 100 of these high quality aircraft in the next few years.

The Red Chinese navy has also undergone a modernization program aimed at producing a "blue water" navy (ie. capable of operating long distances from base for extended periods of time.)

The Red Chinese navy possesses as many as 1700 vessels. Many of these vessels are small, coastal patrol boats. But most of China's naval resources are going to building larger, modern ships. According to the International Institute for Strategic Studies' "Military Balance," Red China already operates 18 destroyers, 36 frigates, and 90 submarines capable of operating far from China's home ports. And China is working feverishly to expand its blue water navy as rapidly as possible.

Red China's new Luhu-class destroyers have been designed and built specifically to help Beijing take control of the sea in a conflict — presumably with the Taiwanese or American navy. According to Andy Sywak of the Center for Defense Information, these warships have modern guided missile systems for air and surface combat and two French Dauphin helicopters for anti-submarine combat.

Supplementing the Chinese-built Luhu destroyers are the Russian Sovremenny-class destroyers bought in 1997 for $800,000,000. The Center for Defense Information contends that these Russian destroyers "significantly bolster [Red China's] long-range offensive capabilities."

Complimenting the destroyer fleet are the Jiangwei-class frigates. They have guided missile systems and sophisticated radar like the Luhu destroyers, and also have high quality sonar for detecting and attacking enemy submarines.

China's submarines are the strongest arm of Beijing's navy. They have several Kilo-class submarines, one of the best diesel submarines in the world, bought from Russia. They have several more nuclear powered Han-class submarines. And the brand new Song-class submarine is just entering service in the Red Chinese fleet. These formidable nuclear powered submarines will soon be the standard attack boat in Beijing's underwater arsenal.

There should be little doubt as to what this modern blue water naval force will be used for. Former *New York*

Times Beijing Bureau Chief Nicholas Kristof predicts that the South China Sea, and specifically Taiwan, will be the most probable place Red China will use its navy. Already, Red China could mount a blockade of Taiwan with its destroyers, frigates, and submarines. And as their navy grows, the possibility increases that Red China could launch an invasion of the island.

The ultimate goal of the Red Chinese navy is to have the ability to contest the United States for control of the seas in the Pacific. Without control of the sea, the massive Red Chinese army could never be brought to bear outside the Chinese mainland. As Beijing's navy continues to grow while the United States continues to reduce its naval presence in Asia, the possibility of the loss of the Pacific to Red China becomes very real.

For the time being, however, the most dire threat China poses to America comes from their nuclear missiles. The Pentagon's top nuclear war-fighter said that "China is engaged in a major nuclear modernization that includes development of multiple-warhead missiles capable of hitting all parts of the U.S. except southern Florida".

Right now, Red China has 18 inter-continental nuclear missiles — 13 of which were pointed at American cities. Red China also has an estimated 70 intermediate range nuclear missiles and 50 medium range nuclear missiles. These missiles present a growing threat to the United States and its allies, and could potentially be used by China to help threaten the nuclear balance with America, as will be discussed in a later chapter. The use of medium range nuclear missiles in tests off of Taiwan in

1995 and 1996 demonstrates China's willingness to use nuclear intimidation against their adversaries.

Just as bad, Red China is helping other enemies of the United States and even terrorist countries develop nuclear missiles of their own. that can be targeted at U.S. troops and citizens. China helped Iran — which calls America the "Great Satan" and held our people hostage for 444 days — build long range Shahab-3 and -4 missiles. They were also caught helping the Iranians with their nuclear development program only weeks after signing an agreement promising not to. China helped North Korea — which started the Korean War that caused over 150,000 American casualties — develop their nuclear missile program. And China helped Pakistan develop the nuclear weapons they tested in May of 1998 in retaliation to an Indian nuclear test — even though they promised not to help Pakistan develop nuclear weapons. Thanks to Red China's proliferation of nuclear technology, the Indian Subcontinent is now the scene of the most tense nuclear stand-off since the Cuban Missile Crisis.

BEIJING CALLS AMERICA THE ENEMY

All the evidence presented so far — the conflict of American and Chinese strategic interests, the tension over Taiwan, building up the military, China's nuclear weapons and proliferation — is convincing enough to most to demonstrate the clear threat Red China poses to the United States. But for those who remain unconvinced, a review of Beijing's own proclamations puts the matter to rest once and for all.

In 1994, a major meeting was held in Beijing's Great Hall of the People. Attending this meeting were high ranking military officials, senior members of the Politburo, propaganda heads of the Communist Party, and representatives from every province of China. Bernstein and Munro report in "The Coming Conflict with China" that the purpose of this major meeting was to "designate the United States as China's main global rival." General Zhang, Chief of the Army General Staff, said:

"Facing blatant interference by the American hegemonists in our internal affairs and their open support for the debilitating activities of hostile elements inside our country and hostile forces outside the mainland and overseas opposing and subverting our socialist system, we must reinforce the Armed Forces more intensively."

This meeting represented an official and open shift in Red China's policy toward the United States, a shift that was entirely instigated by the Chinese. American policy in Asia has been consistent in the 20th Century -to prevent one power from controlling all of Asia. The focus of this policy changed over the years, from European colonialists to Japan to the Soviet Union. But the policy remained the same. And this American policy was not in conflict with China's interests for most of the century. Only since the fall of the Soviet Union has this American policy rankled Red China, because they now see an opportunity to dominate Asia themselves. A senior analyst at the Chinese Society for Strategy and Management Research in Beijing said it openly:

> "China is growing stronger in the world, and that is affecting the dominant role of the United States ... a fundamental conflict will be inevitable. (Bernstein and Munro, *The Coming Conflict with China*)"

To that end, the Red Chinese military has been preparing for a conflict with the United States. A secret 1993 Red Chinese Army report called "Can the Chinese Army Win the Next War?" shows that war with America is the focus of Chinese military planning. The report even goes so far as to conclude that:

> "China and the United States, focused on their respective economic and political interests in the Asia-Pacific region, will remain in a sustained state of confrontation."

As Bernstein and Munro state in their book: "Rarely have Chinese statements been so explicit about the United States being a strategic foe of China, but the idea of the United States as an enemy is far from new."

Red China's view of America as their prime enemy (rather than the Soviet Union) can be traced to the Tianaman Square Massacre in 1989. The Communist leadership in Beijing suspected that the United States inspired and sponsored the pro-democracy student uprising that threatened their power. They pointed to the symbol of the uprising, the Goddess of Democracy, which was a replica of the Statue of Liberty. And when the U.S. suspended high level contacts with Beijing after the crackdown and offered asylum for any student protester who escaped from China, the Communist Party leadership was convinced America was behind the uprising.

A second major historical event which caused a shift in Red China's view of the United States came from the fall of the Soviet Empire from 1989-1992. The Soviet Union had been the biggest threat to China's security since the 1960's, and the majority of their military was focused on countering the Russian military. When the Soviet Union collapsed and the military threat from Russia diminished, it freed up the bulk of Red China's military for other duties.

The fall of the Soviet Union also taught the communists in China a very important lesson. Attempts to reform the communist system and ease government oppression, as Gorbachev tried to do in the Soviet Union, led to disaster. The leadership in Beijing is determined not to let that happen to them. And they view the United States as the major source of outside instigation and interference causing unrest in China.

The final major event which caused Red China to change its attitude to the United States was the Persian Gulf War in 1991. The awesome military power demonstrated by the United States let Red China know just how far behind they were in military doctrine, technology, and operations. Based on the results of the Gulf War, the Chinese knew that they would lose if they came into conflict with the United States. This realization gave new focus to the Chinese military, prompting modernization programs, changes in tactics, and operational adjustments. Evidence of this change can be seen in the development of Red China's missile program. They made a massive effort to improve their long range nuclear missiles so they could credibly threaten the United States. And they embarked on new medium range missile programs, the likes of which were tested off of Taiwan in 1996.

CONCLUSION

Red China is America's primary enemy in the world. China's goal of domination of Asia is in direct conflict with America's policy of preventing one country from dominating Asia. And China's specific goal of recapturing Taiwan, America's ally, puts them on a collision course with the United States.

The overwhelming weight of evidence also indicates that Red China's military is doing everything it can to prepare for a war with the United States. They are modernizing their army and adding accurate missiles to their arsenal to increase firepower. They are buying or building every top of the line attack aircraft they can manage. And they are rapidly expanding their blue water navy to project power far from their coastal waters.

Finally, the leadership in Beijing has said for themselves, in their own documents and announcements, that America is their enemy. The 1994 conference in Beijing made it clear that Red China's official policy was to consider the U.S. their "main global rival". And their secret military documents prove that Red China's armed forces are practicing and preparing for a war with the United States of America.

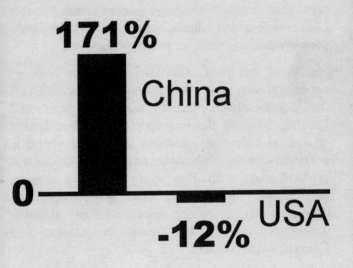

171%

China

0

-12% USA

Percentage change in military spending for the United States and Red China, 1993-1998.

Considering this, the developments at the Panama Canal since 1997 should give our leaders in Washington, D.C. cause for great alarm. Because it appears that, as part of their plan to dominate Asia, Red China is moving to take over the world's most vital strategic waterway-the Panama Canal.

When we say "take over" we want to be very clear on one thing. If Red China is the "Gatekeeper" of the Panama Canal because she controls the entrance-exit ports that govern who enters and exits the Panama Canal, only a Bill Clinton trained semanticist could possibly confuse what we mean by takeover.

As of this publication date, there has been no opposition party response to the policy (or lack thereof) that is currently in place by the United States and Panama. Most of the major opinion leaders I have spoken to either are unaware there is a problem, uncertain of what can be done, or in full denial that this problem exists at all. This failure to respond to easily ascertainable facts (or this acquiescence to developments) is much more of an alarming development once viewed through the prism of Red China strategic concerns.

II. DECEMBER 31, 1999: USA OUT, RED CHINA IN

In 1903, Panama proclaimed its independence from Colombia and was immediately recognized by the United States. Shortly thereafter, Panama and the United States agreed to allow America to begin building a Canal in exchange for ten million dollars up front and $250,000 a year after that.

There has never been any question that, except for the early involvement of the United States in the life of Panama, there would not have been an independent country called Panama.

The President of the United States recognized the urgent need for a Panama Canal, and he helped the patriots who became Panama's founding fathers, declare their independence. In this, he did no more, and no less, than the French and other foreigners who helped make the difference in our own United States War of Independence.

So from the very beginning of existence of the country of Panama, a friendship and cooperation has existed between the two nations. A friendship and cooperation based upon the foundation of the Panama Canal and the importance of its continued operation.

Anti-American revisionists in Panama who constantly prattle on about the "reverted territories" that the United States is at long last giving back to Panama, should consider their nation's history a little more accurately. If we truly wanted the properties to revert, perhaps we should revert them back to Columbia, where they came from.

There were major problems in construction of the Canal. Those problems included engineering problems and health problems. Our purpose here is not to pay tribute to those great Americans who built what many call the Eighth Wonder of the World, but we do want to note the significance of this unique achievement.

Actual construction of the Canal began in 1904. Many Americans (and other nationals, including Panamanians) died building this Canal. Finally, by the summer of 1914, the Canal was open to limited use.

Almost immediately, the Panama Canal proved its vital strategic role when the United States entered the First World War in 1917. Shipping critical to the war effort passed through the newly opened Canal, which helped turn the tide against Nazi Germany.

The Canal was officially opened to all traffic in 1920, sparking an era of economic prosperity in Panama. However, internal political chaos often threatened the Canal in the 1920's. Anti-American nationalists began demanding control of the Panama Canal and threatened the Americans administering it. Then, a revolutionary group hostile to the United States took control of Panama in 1931, leading to years of antagonistic U.S.-Panamanian relations and constant worry for the safety of the Canal.

After years of dispute, America and Panama signed a new Panama Canal Treaty in 1936 which permitted the United States to intervene militarily to safeguard the

Canal in return for commercial rights for Panama. Fortunately, this new Treaty came before the Second World War, so America had stability at this strategic choke point during that great conflict.

In the post-war period, Panama's economy stagnated. Thinking the Canal a cure-all, extremists began to demand that America surrender the profitable Canal to Panama, especially after Egypt took the Suez Canal from England in 1956. In 1959 anti-American rallies were held and repeated attempts were made to invade the Canal Zone. Extremist agitation culminated in riots in 1964 that had to be quelled by American troops to keep the Canal safe.

The 1960's were dominated by constant left-wing carping on the continuing theme that other countries detested the United States. This author came of age politically during this period in which the singular policy prescription for all foreign policy ills, is that the United States is bad, and should withdraw. The Communists of Hanoi, North Vietnam, tremendously benefited from having a strong leftwing contingent conducting regular "Moratorium" anti-war protests during this period. But the anti-U.S.A. leftists in Panama benefited from this work by their American cousins and ideological soulmates also. The difference is that in the United States, many of us put up a struggle to counter the left in their demand that we abandon our friends in Vietnam. But no such struggle to help our pro-USA, anti-leftist friends in Panama ever took place in America.

Consequently, by the late 1960's, the United States and Panama began to negotiate new Panama Canal Treaties. Negotiations continued under Republican Presidents. But the national security needs of the United States always seemed to tilt the United States against a final agreement. Until, that is, the advent of liberal Democrat Jimmy Carter as President. The same Carter who signed an unconditional pardon for the 10,000 Vietnam era draft-dodgers, also put America's national security needs and the needs of our friends on the back burner in Panama. Carter gave in to the demands of Panama dictator Omar Torrijos and signed two new Panama Canal Treaties in 1977. These treaties provided for the giveaway of the Panama Canal at the end of 1999.

The Panama Canal Treaties were widely opposed by the American people. As a Reagan for President fieldman in 1976 I can testify to this firsthand. When Ronald Reagan talked about the Panama Canal we were flooded with donations and volunteers. Later I helped form an organization to fight the giveaway of the Panama Canal and we enjoyed massive support. Despite this overwhelming public opposition, the treaties were rammed through the Senate in 1978. But for the first time, a line had been drawn. No longer could the left operate with impunity and with no response from the conservative side.

Meanwhile, back in Panama, the military continued its corrupt and unlawful control of the country throughout the 1980's, under General Manuel Noriega. But in 1988 General Noriega was defeated for reelection by the people of Panama. He was also indicted by an American court for drug trafficking. The increasingly belligerent Noriega stood defiant. American soldiers were shot at. Several were killed. The situation at the Panama Canal deteriorated quickly and Dictator Noriega seemed determined to kick the U.S. out. The elected leaders of Panama—blocked from office by the Dictator - appealed to the United States to honor its treaty obligations and intervene to restore calm and stability. In America, there were the usual cast of characters suggesting that more talk was the only way to end the impasse threatening the Panama Canal. But this time, there was no repeat of the usual cycle of demands by the American left to completely give in to whatever the anti-USA despots of Panama wanted, with a deafening silence from American conservatives. This time, it was very obvious to all, there was a public base of support for a defense of America interests at the Panama Canal. This time, it was very obvious, that there was a base of support to stand by our friends.

And so in December of 1989, "Operation Just Cause" was ordered by President George Bush, with 24,000 U.S. troops sent in to Panama. As we conservatives had said all along, starting with Ronald Reagan in 1976, standing up for American interests at the Panama Canal would be politically popular. The American troops had a simple goal: oust Dictator Noriega and protect the Canal from terrorist attack, under terms of the Neutrality Treaty which provides that the U.S. can defend the Canal against any threat.

Instead of anti-USA demonstrations that American liberals predicted, the new heroes to Panamanians were the American troops who restored order and who were seen patrolling on every street corner. I was told by American commanders on my recent visit to Panama, that the military bases at the Panama Canal enabled our forces to neutralize every military target within six hours of being given the "kick-off" command by the President. And they also confirmed that this could never have happened without launching from military bases within Panama. Operating from offshore aircraft carriers and support vessels would have extended the six hour window and increased the casualty rate enormously.

The U.S. "Operation Just Cause" saved the Canal for the time being, but the long history of Panama indicated that a new leftist, anti-USA threat to this vital strategic waterway will rise again.

This new threat emerged in 1997 when Red China moved to take over the Panama Canal ports of Balboa and Cristobal. But this time, it appears that the United States has reverted to its old policy of appeasement at worst, or acquiescence at best. This time, the United States has not reacted to preserve its security interests. At this writing, there has not even been a protest by the opposition party to the President for this lack of a policy to counter alarming developments at Panama.

Before we spell out how U.S. interests are once again under attack in Panama, it is important to fully understand the role of naval power and the Panama Canal in the development of the United States.

NAVAL POWER & THE PANAMA CANAL

Alfred Thayer Mahan, in many ways the father of the modern American Navy, helped the United States emerge as a world power in the late 1800's. His writings guided the American Navy from a coastal defense navy to a blue water, capital ship navy. And with this capital ship navy, the United States began to assert itself on the world stage — even to the point of displacing a European nation (Spain) and acquiring its territories in the Caribbean and the Pacific Ocean.

The development of a legitimate capital ship navy was the first crucial step in the U.S. role in what has been called the "American Century". As Mahan pointed out, the most important single element to a country's greatness — indeed, the root of national power — comes from sea communications and trade. And the only way to protect and control seaborne communications and trade is to have a dominant capital ship navy and a coherent naval strategy.

Mahan made three very important points about a naval strategy that would allow United States to assert its dominance in the world. First, a massive merchant marine must be in place to accommodate international trade. The more American goods sold abroad, the stronger the U.S. economy becomes. And cheaper imported raw materials would give American businesses a competitive edge.

Second, a great navy must be built to protect this merchant marine and project power. This great navy must, first and foremost, be able to engage and destroy enemy fleets which could threaten friendly shipping. Once the threat from enemy fleets is dealt with, the navy can then go on to secondary missions, such as enemy merchant interdiction and littoral warfare in support of ground operations.

Third and finally, the United States must be in control of the Panama Canal to control the interior lines of communication and transport. This canal would help solve one of the most vexing problems in U.S. naval strategy. Before the Panama Canal was built, the United States was forced to maintain two separate navies — one in the Atlantic and one in the Pacific. Thus, America was incapable of bringing all of its naval firepower to bear in one ocean. So, while the American navy as a whole was on par with the other great navies, it was weakened by the fact that it was split in two. Until a canal could be built, American naval power would never be dominant in the world.

President Theodore Roosevelt understood this, and made it his mission to see that a canal was built to solve this problem.

The Panama Canal was vital to American security for the rest of this century. The Second World War would have dragged on months, even years longer if the United States hadn't controlled the Panama Canal. And the Canal gave the United States a strategic advantage in the Korean War, the Cuban Missile Crisis, the Vietnam War, and the Persian Gulf War, to name a few. In each case, thanks to the Panama Canal the United States was able to bring more ships and troops to the conflict more quickly. And just imagine how important the Canal would have been in the event of a Soviet invasion of Western Europe during the Cold War.

BIG TROUBLE IN PANAMA

Admiral Thomas Moorer, former Chairman of the Joint Chiefs of Staff, calls the Panama Canal the most vital strategic waterway in the world. Admiral Moorer testified before the Senate Foreign Relations Committee in 1998 about the current U.S. policy towards Panama and the Canal, ". . . we are on what I consider to be a collision course with disaster in the very near future." He goes on to testify, "I see big trouble in Panama-trouble that could evolve quickly into a conflict in our own hemisphere with world-wide implications" (complete text available from National Security Center).

Over 12,500 commercial vessels transit the Panama Canal every year, carrying more than 164 million metric tons of cargo. The Canal cuts 8,000 miles off the trip from the Atlantic Ocean to the Pacific Ocean saving our merchant ships billions of dollars in fuel and lost time.

The Panama Canal is also critical for the U.S. Navy. Thanks to the Panama Canal, the U.S. Navy can cut two full weeks of steaming time to respond to a crisis in Europe, the Middle East, or even Cuba.

In fact, if it weren't for our Panama Canal, the United States may never have avoided an atomic showdown with the Soviet Union during the 1962 Cuban Missile Crisis. It was only because our U.S. Navy could quickly sail through our Panama Canal to the shores of Cuba that Khrushchev was forced to negotiate with President Kennedy.

And during the Vietnam War our Panama Canal was absolutely critical to supplying the war effort in Asia. More than 90% of all military supplies and soldiers were transported to Vietnam by ship — and 65% of those transported went through the Panama Canal.

The Panama Canal's vital importance hasn't diminished since Vietnam either. It was just as important in the Persian Gulf War. And the Canal will continue to play a vital role far into the next century.

There are several critical military bases which the United States must continue to operate into the 21st Century. Howard Air Force Base, on the Pacific side, is a 5,300 acre all-weather jet air base and home of the 24th Air Wing of the U.S. Air Force, operating attack aircraft, helicopters, transports, surveillance AWACs and cargo planes. It has an 8,000 foot runway, strong enough to handle any plane that flies. Troops from Howard Air Force Base engage in drug interdiction, air traffic operations, rescue missions and pilot training. Howard Air Force Base is the largest and most important U.S. base south of the Rio Grande.

Rodman Naval Station, also on the Pacific side, is a deep-draft port facility capable of handling any warship for logistic support in supplies, fueling and repairs.

Fort Sherman, on the Atlantic side, is unique in that it is the only base in the world specializing in jungle warfare and survivor training. As with Howard AFB and Rodman NS, Fort Sherman is another magnifent military installation, developed by dedicated professionals, loyal to their mission and proficient in its execution.

Galeta Island, also on the Atlantic side, is a very important intelligence-collecting and code- breaking facility for SOUTHCOM, indeed for the United States. Many details of its operations are classified, but it is known that the location is unique in its geological properties for underwater communication in both the Atlantic and Pacific Oceans and for collecting important intelligence.

Quarry Heights Headquarters for SOUTHCOM is a well-established and fully outfitted facility, sitting on Ancon Hill in Panama near the Gorgas Army Hospital and Ancon Hill Communications antenna array.

Finally, Ancon Hill Communications is SOUTHCOM's million-dollar antenna arrays on top of Ancon Hill, visible for miles around and capable of world-spanning communications.

III. RED CHINA'S MAN TAKES CANAL PORTS

Li Ka-shing is the billionaire Chairman of Hutchison Whampoa and an extremely powerful Hong Kong business tycoon. But Li Ka-shing is much more than that. Li is also one of the most trusted allies of the Communist Chinese government. And he is masterminding the takeover of the Panama Canal for Red China. Today, he controls ports in Panama and just offshore of the Eastern United States, the Bahamas. His influence is quiet, but decisive. Shortly after his company took over in the Bahamas, that country withdrew its recognition of Free China, and recognized Red China.

In fact, Li Ka-shing has a long standing relationship with Red China's brutal communist dictatorship, dating back to the 1970's with Deng Xioaping.

In his biography, *Li Ka-shing: Hong Kong's Elusive Billionaire,* Anthony B. Chan clearly documents the extremely close ties Li Ka-shing and Red China have with one another.

On April 28, 1992 Li received an honorary degree from Red China's Beijing University. Granting the honors upon Li was none other than Jiang Zemin, the current dictator of Red China. As Mr. Chan puts it:

> "The symbolic gesture of making public what in private any China-watcher had long known – that even Beijing was capable of loving the

most revered capitalist in Hong Kong." (*Li Ka-shing*, p.1)

The leaders of *Communist* China "loving" a capitalist from Hong Kong? How could that possibly be?

Simple. Li Ka-shing and the communist leaders in Beijing are close allies who work together in the business world -and the political world. As Mr. Chan explains:

> "Li was the vital go between that the geriatric bosses of Beijing needed to firm up the support of Hong Kong's other leading merchants in the smooth recovery of the colony to China in 1997." (*Li Ka-shing*, p.3-4)

Li was used by the Red Chinese to help them take over Hong Kong without firing a shot. And the communists knew they could count on their ally, because Li "understood his place in the Chinese scheme of things. He never showed distress over Tiananmin ... or castigated Beijing for its actions. As Li later explained: 'I was of course saddened [by the Tiananmin massacre]. But as a Chinese China is my motherland. No matter what happened, I am still willing to work for the future of my country.'" (*Li Ka-shing*, p.5)

Clearly, from this statement alone, Li Ka-shing is in the back pocket of Red China. And he has been a close ally of Beijing for some time now. The Red Chinese began courting Li as far back as 1977, when he was an up and coming businessman in Hong Kong. In

1979, Li became a member of Red China's CITIC, a government economic agency. "For Li, an appointment to Beijing's top investment arm was nothing short of an honor." (*Li Ka-shing*, p.6) It was also nothing short of permanently allying himself with Red China.

Li has always denied that his membership in the CITIC made him a Red Chinese agent. But the evidence proves otherwise.

For Li, "association with Chinese power brokers had swayed the Hong Kong Bank to sell him his share of Hutchison Whampoa, and that with expansive commercial clout in Hong Kong and strong political connections in Beijing his power could only increase." (*Li Ka-shing*, p.6)

Li Ka-shing owes a lot to Red China. They helped him become a powerful man in Hong Kong. And they helped him acquire the corporation that made him a billionaire.

Red China has benefited enormously from bringing Li Ka-shing into their fold. Li has spent a fortune supporting Red China with investments and construction contracts. And he has donated millions of dollars to Red China for charity.

Li has also helped Red China improve their shipping infrastructure. Hutchison Whampoa is the only company that Red China trusts to run its commercial ports, and is virtually running south China's seaborne trade. A *Journal of Commerce* report by Joe Studwell

Li Ka-shing, Chairman of Hutchison Whampoa.

even reported that Hutchison Whampoa has a "cozy relationship" with Red China that is as "close as lips and teeth".

Most importantly, Li was used by the Red Chinese to help their takeover of Hong Kong in 1997. Li was picked by Beijing to be a member of their Preparatory Committee charged with overseeing the takeover. This Committee's first task? The "wholesale elimination of Hong Kong's first and recently elected sixty seat legislature," to be replaced by a "puppet body" appointed by Red China. (*Li Ka-shing*, p.212)

It is evident from Mr. Chan's biography of Li Ka-shing alone that he is a close ally of Red China. But there are many other sources which document Li Ka-shing's ties to Red China. In fact, there is a parade of evidence in magazines, journals, and newspapers from across the world documenting the ties between Hutchison Whampoa and Red China. Here is just a sampling.

Nikkei Weekly (March 2, 1998): Red China is "looking to reach into the pockets of Hong Kong business leaders for funds to keep the Chinese economy rolling". Li Ka-shing, who has "close connections to the mainland" is "undoubtedly on Beijing's list of potential cash suppliers". It also reports that Li Ka-shing has "tried to secure CPPCC membership [Chinese People's Political Consultative Conference] for his eldest son and heir apparent, Victor Li Tzar-Kuoi, to keep contacts with the top brass in Beijing".

Nikkei Weekly also reports that Li Ka-shing "converted to the pro-China camp in the late 1980's" and "started establishing close relations with the family of Deng Xiaoping by helping Chinese companies affiliated with the People's Liberation Army enter the Hong Kong market".

Finally, this periodical makes the point that, to do business in China, "the name of the game is connections". Li Ka-shing has been doing business in China by "making huge donations and building connections" in Communist China.

Asian Political News (October 13, 1997): Li Ka-shing actually "posted congratulatory messages" in a new daily Hong Kong newspaper operated by the Red Chinese after the communist takeover of the city. Thanking his friends in the tyrannical communist regime for taking over free and democratic Hong Kong?

The Independent of London (July 1, 1997): When Red Chinese leaders came to Hong Kong to oversee their takeover of the city from Great Britain, Li Ka-shing rolled out the red carpet for them. Communist China's leader, Jiang Zemin, stayed at one of Li's hotels during the takeover. Zemin and Red China's other leaders chose to dine at Li's hotel rather than attend the dinner the British had prepared for them. And in the final ceremony for the Red Chinese takeover of Hong Kong, Li Ka-shing stood with Red China's Jiang Zemin. *The Independent* did note that Li Ka-shing did not attend morning celebrations because "he is a target for pro-democracy activists".

The Guardian, also of London (June 11, 1997): "So powerful is this nexus of contract-hungry tycoons and politically potent Chinese leaders that even governments on the other side of the world must reckon with their clout. A recent decision by the Bahamas to sever diplomatic relations with Taiwan and establish ties with Beijing is widely thought to have been motivated by concern over a newly opened port run by Hutchison Whampoa, Ltd., a Hong Kong conglomerate controlled by Mr. Li, the pro-China mogul." If that isn't clear, damning evidence of Red Chinese control over Hutchison Whampoa, then what is?

Asian Business (March, 1997): "Li has taught his sons, Victor and Richard, the importance of good contacts with top leaders, such as Chinese president Jiang Zemin."

Regarding Li Ka-shing's support for Red China's plans to administer Hong Kong, *Asian Business* quotes Li directly: "Yes, I strongly believe in what they say."

And Li is assured a place at the epicenter of power in Red China's Hong Kong. "He is an advisor on Hong Kong affairs to the Beijing government and has served on the Selection Committee that picked Tung Chee-hwa" as the leader of Hong Kong. This leader displaced the democratically elected leadership in Hong Kong when Red China took over and rules for Beijing.

The Financial Times reported (March 13, 1998): Li Ka-shing has a picture of Communist China's leader, Jiang Zemin, in his office.

Agence France Presse (February 20-21, 1997): Li Ka-shing publicly mourned the death of Red China's former leader, Deng Xiaoping, the day after he died. At the same time, a "small group of demonstrators staged a demonstration against Deng Xiaoping". One demonstrator asked "why do people mourn him today, and not remember" that Deng ordered the troops to massacre the peaceful protesters at Tianamin Square.

Agence France Presse (November 12, 1996): "Chinese leaders have called Li a 'patriot' for his charitable work and his 20 billion Hong Kong dollars of investments in the mainland. He is a vice-chairman of the committee set up by Beijing to form a post-1997 Hong Kong government."

Sunday Times (June 30, 1996): "The Chinese communist leaders turned for help to the benevolent figure of a Hong Kong property billionaire, Li Ka-shing."

Agence France Presse (April 28, 1997)): Hutchison Whampoa "is a partner with China Ocean Shipping Company (COSCO) in several enterprises in China and elsewhere in Asia." COSCO is an arm of the People's Liberation Army and is totally controlled by the communist government.

Journal of Commerce (March 26, 1997): An unidentified State Department spokesman "noted that Hutchison has ventures in Asia with state-run China Ocean Shipping Company."

"Hutchison did operate two of its berths at Hong Kong's Terminal 8 in 50-50 partnership with COSCO

Pacific, Ltd., the local arm of China's main shipping company."

USA Today (January 13, 1998): Companies wanting to do business in China would be served well to cozy up to Li Ka-shing. A company called Peregrine leveraged "their close ties to Hong Kong billionaire Li Ka-shing to gain the trust of Chinese leaders."

The Kentucky Post (October 24, 1997): Proctor & Gamble Co. chairman and chief executive said "Hutchison has been and will continue to be a valuable partner in building our business in China.

These are but a few quotes from sources around the world documenting the close ties between Li Ka-shing's Hutchison Whampoa and Red China. And they demonstrate unequivocally two things:

1) The close business partnership between Hutchison Whampoa and Red China would not occur if Li wasn't willing to toe the line with the communist's political agenda. Hutchison virtually controls all the ports in southern China. Hutchison is partners with Red China's shipping company, which is controlled by the People's Liberation Army. Foreign investors seeking to do business in China go through Li Ka-shing. And Li provides Beijing with billions of dollars worth of services and desperately needed hard currency to the Red Chinese government. You don't do that kind of business in China unless they absolutely trust you.

2) Li has demonstrated his subservience to the communist leadership in China and his willingness to do the bidding of Beijing. He publicly mourned the death of the Butcher of Tianamin Square, Deng Xiaoping. He helped the communists appoint their cronies to displace the democratically elected legislature of Hong Kong and made their takeover of in 1997 as easy as possible. And the reports that the Bahamas cut ties to Taiwan and established an embassy with Red China because Hutchison Whampoa took over a port there indicate Li Ka-shing's willingness to use his economic muscle to help his communist allies in Beijing.

Conclusion

Hutchison is not just a group of Chinese businessmen. You don't get to be the size of this company when you operate in Red China, without operating as an arm of the government. Americans who don't understand this are either very naïve and uninformed, or have the same hardcore leftist, anti-USA agenda of the anti-Vietnam marchers of the 1960's. Li Ka-shing was not given the opportunity to run the ports of Red China because he gave the best bid in the sense that we Americans think companies operate. His "best bid" to Red China is actually a total package that includes loyalty to the policy goals of Red China. Li ka-shing is doing his finest work for Red China in Panama.

IV. A SINISTER PLOT

It has been evident since the Panama Canal Treaties were signed in 1977 that the Panamanian government was incapable of efficiently running the Canal facilities without continued assistance. Inefficient operations and excessively high prices charged by the Panamanian government prevented it. The 1996 Army Corps of Engineers Report (available from National Security Center) detailed the neglect of the Panama Canal by the government of Panama. Captain Evans has documented the deterioration of the Canal in his book, *Death Knell of the Panama Canal?* (also available from NSC).

To deal with this problem, the Panamanian government decided to bring in private companies to maintain Canal facilities and keep them in good condition. Since the 1994 election of President Ernesto Perez Balladares, privatization of the Canal facilities handed over to them by the United States has been a top priority.

The Panamanian government began discussions with several companies regarding contracts to run the key ports of Balboa on the Pacific and Cristobal on the Atlantic. It was always the Panamanians intention to negotiate these base rights separately, to make sure no one company had control of ports on both sides of the Canal (in fact, Balboa is the only port on the Pacific side of the Canal).

In June 1995, Panamanian officials signed a letter of agreement to let Kawasaki, a Japanese firm, and its American subsidiary, I.T.S., take over the port of

Balboa. Another American firm, Bechtel, also expressed an interest in investing $600-700 million in the Canal, specifically the ports of Balboa and Cristobal and the isthmus railroad.

But seeing a golden opportunity to secure the Panama Canal for his Red Chinese masters, in stepped Li Ka-shing. Agents for Hutchison Whampoa immediately began talks with Panamanian officials about taking over both the Balboa and Cristobal ports, and the railroad which connects them across the Isthmus of Panama. Rather than honor their previous agreements with Kawasaki/I.T.S., Panamanian officials commissioned "studies" to find out exactly how much these ports and the railroad were worth. But what it appears they were really doing was stalling to see what kind of deal they could arrange for themselves with Hutchison Whampoa.

In the spring of 1996, their study was done and the Panamanians were ready to begin accepting new bids for the ports — despite the fact that they already had an agreement with Kawasaki/I.T.S. The initial bidding process on June 3 was chaotic and confused, with various companies offering new bids each time they found out what others had submitted. So the Panamanians held a second round of bidding on June 18th.

In this second round of bidding, Bechtel, Kawasaki/I.T.S. and M.I.T. (a Panamanian/American company) had the most competitive bids. Even some Panamanian officials admitted that M.I.T. had the best overall offer. Hutchison Whampoa was judged to have come in fourth out of the five bidders.

But Dr. Gabriel Castro, Panama's National Security Advisor, asked M.I.T. to withdraw their bid. Because M.I.T. already controlled one of the ports on the Atlantic side, the addition of both the Balboa and Cristobal ports would give them a near monopoly. (Never mind that Hutchison Whampoa also bid for both the Balboa and Cristobal ports, and that control of Balboa alone would give them a monopoly on the Pacific side.)

When Hutchison Whampoa found out they were not even in the running for the contract, they approached Panamanian officials and offered to double their bid to get the ports. At first, they were told it was too late. Soon after, however, the Panamanians decided to hold yet another round of bidding to give Hutchison Whampoa a chance to submit their doubled offer.

Was it this "better offer" that made the Panamanians change their mind? Or was it what Panamanian opposition Congressman Leopoldo Benedetti told me while I was in Panama, "Bucket loads of money from Asian contractors are pouring in." Everyone I spoke to in Panama told me the same thing - that there is a lot of money going "under the table" but that it is hard to prove anything since the investigators were appointed by the people they are investigating, and that means brothers, relatives, friends, cronies and political hacks are in charge of investigating other brothers, relatives, friends, cronies and political hacks.

On July 3rd a third round of bidding commenced, with specific conditions set up to make it easier for Hutchison Whampoa to win, forcing several bidders out right away. American Ambassador Hughes protested the conditions of the bidding, noting that the conditions significantly favored one company (Hutchison Whampoa). Bechtel and I.T.S. each complained that the bidding process was being manipulated to make sure Hutchison Whampoa won. Bechtel withdrew its original bid in protest.

Hutchison Whampoa and I.T.S. were the only ones left to submit bids. Hutchison's offer of $22.2 million annually more than doubled I.T.S., and Hutchison Whampoa won the contract to take control of the ports of Balboa and Cristobal. American Ambassador Hughes protested the bidding process yet again, but was "scolded" by Panamanian officials for it.

But what of the concern by the Panamanians that no one company get a port monopoly at the Canal? National Security Advisor Gabriel Castro told M.I.T. to withdraw their bid so they wouldn't get a monopoly of the ports. How different was it when Hutchison Whampoa took over Cristobal, one of only three ports on the Atlantic side of the Canal, and Balboa, the only port on the Pacific side?

RODMAN NAVAL STATION

M.I.T. was told, as compensation for withdrawing their bid for Balboa and Cristobal, that Panama would consider letting them develop a port facility at Rodman Naval Station when the U.S. withdraws in 1999. (Development of a port before the U.S. withdraws, both Panama and the United States claim, would interfere with the U.S. Navy's operations there.) In mid-1996 negotiations began for M.I.T. to take over operation of Rodman after the U.S. withdraws.

One condition of the negotiations from M.I.T. was that the Panamanian government not tell Hutchison Whampoa about the potential deal. A letter of intent was drafted, stating:

> "The State (Panama) declares that, while negotiations are in progress, it will not undertake any negotiations with other companies with respect to the port facility described in the First clause of this letter of intent, referring to the intentions declared by both the State and Panama Pacific Terminal (PPT) in designing, constructing, and operation a modern and efficient port facility for containers in the area north of the Port of Rodman."

But a member of the M.I.T. consortium told Hutchison Whampoa officials about this letter of intent. Hutchison offered a sweetheart deal to this member to switch sides and join with them in an attempt to take over the U.S. Navy's Rodman Naval Station. Then Hutchison went to the Panamanian government and told them M.I.T.'s intent to take over Rodman was a "deal breaker". They then threatened to pull their $22.2 million a year bid for Balboa and Cristobal if they weren't given the right of first refusal for Rodman. The Panamanian government, fearing to lose the millions Hutchison would bring them, caved in and nullified the agreement with M.I.T. Hutchison got their right of first refusal for three years. (This right of first refusal is standard operating procedure for Hutchison Whampoa. According to the Journal of Commerce, Hutchison also "cut a deal with the Ministry of Communication [of Red China] giving them first right of refusal over all coastal ports south of Yangtze River".) M.I.T. was shut out and has lost hundreds of thousands of dollars they already spent in preparation for their takeover of Rodman.

HUTCHISON WHAMPOA TAKES OVER

In March of 1997, the government of Panama officially handed over control of the American built piers and port facilities at Balboa and Cristobal to Hutchison Whampoa and its chairman, Li Ka-shing — effectively handing control of these ports to Red China.

And thanks to this agreement, Hutchison Whampoa now has the right of first refusal for the key American naval station at Rodman. Hutchison Whampoa has also been given long term "options" for other facilities, including several other military installations the United States is evacuating.

This contract which gave Hutchison control of the Canal ports and other "rights" is spelled out in detail in the government of Panama's Law No. 5, passed on January 16th by Panama's Legislative Assembly. Panama made its deal with Hutchison Whampoa without consultation with the United States, in some respects in violation of the 1977 Panama Canal Treaties and its own Constitution.

Law No. 5 was passed by Panama's Legislative Assembly on January 16, 1997 and published in the "Official Gazette" on January 21st, at which time it became law. A careful reading of this law should jolt our leaders in the State Department, the White House and the Congress. Of particular concern, of course, is the part which surrenders the strategic ports of Balboa and Cristobal. Indeed, it was a jolt for the members of the Merchant Marine Panel of the House Committee on National Security, including Chairman Herbert Bateman, R-VA, and ranking member Gene Taylor, D-MS, when Captain Evans brought it to their attention.

Law No. 5 is called a "contract" for operating the ports of Balboa and Cristobal, but it really is much more. It is also a long-term plan for shocking concessions and usurpation of unwarranted authority after the Americans are scheduled to depart on December 31, 1999 (the U.S. surrender date under the Panama Canal Treaties).

Who did the unorthodox negotiating which led to Law No. 5 and the usurpation of authority to allies of Communist China? One negotiator was Hugo Torrijos, nephew of the late dictator Omar Torrijos, the man who signed the Panama Canal Treaties without constitutional authority. Hugo's Panamanian negotiating partner was Minister of Commerce Raul Casteazoro Arango, a member of one of the fourteen "ruling families" of Panama.

Negotiating for Hutchison Whampoa was the prestigious Panamanian Law firm of Morgan and Morgan. One of the Morgan partners is Eduardo Morgan, currently Ambassador to the U.S. Ambassador Morgan took umbrage in *The Washington Times* to a column by Captain Evans exposing the confusion in

Panama in trying to "dispose" of the $32 billion worth of U.S. taxpayer property soon to drop in Panama's lap.

Anyway, there are many aspects of Law No. 5 that are very secretive and very interesting:

• It received very little publicity, apparently because the Panamanian people are strongly anti-Communist and would react harshly to their government handing over control of the ports to allies of Red China (Panama recognizes Free China, not Red China)!

• Panama's leading newspaper *La Prensa* had virtually nothing to say on the matter. Publisher Roberto Eisenmann admitted to me that he opposes any U.S. presence in Panama after 1999. So I can see why he didn't sound any alarms when Law No. 5 passed.

• TV Channel 4, owned by former Foreign Minister Fernando Eleta, laughed, when I asked him about Red China's moving in as the new Gatekeeper of the Panama Canal. So of course Channel 4 was silent.

• Law No. 5 is called a "Concessions and Investment Contract," but it is obviously more than just a business deal when it comes to operating the Panama Canal. In fact, Law No. 5 violates Article 274 of the Panamanian Constitution which requires a plebiscite on Panama Canal matters. None was held.

• The law in Article 2.lld of Law No. 5 violates the guarantee of "expedited treatment" of U.S. warships agreed to in Article VI and Amendment (2) of the Panama Neutrality Treaty by denying use of port facilities if such use would interfere with Hutchison Whampoa's operations.

- Hutchison Whampoa goes by the name of "Panama Ports Company" in Law No. 5, apparently a cover-up so the Panamanian people will not connect Hutchison with the Communist Chinese.

Apparently, the Panamanian government felt that they could bypass portions of the Panama Canal Treaties that restrict their unfettered use of the Canal facilities profitable to them. In the same vein, Panamanian President Ernesto "Toro" Balladares agreed with President Clinton on September 6th, 1995 in the Oval Office to hold exploratory talks for base rights negotiations. The talks never happened. Instead, President Balladares scoured Europe and Asia for money-making deals for the U.S. bases and other properties being surrendered in 1999.

President Balladares was reported "happy to sign" Law No. 5.

Some of the shocking provisions of this hush-hush law, as it pertains to U.S. security, give Hutchison Whampoa and their Communist Chinese allies many "rights" that are potentially disastrous to America:

- Article 2.1 grants Hutchison Whampoa the option of controlling Diablo (town site) and Telfers Island, the latter a potential monitoring site for Galeta Island, the strategic U.S. communications station on the Atlantic side. With it the communists could spy on us!

- Article 2.1 also allows a monopoly for Hutchison Whampoa against any competition at Diablo and Telfers Island.

• Article 2.1 further grants "first option" to Hutchison Whampoa to take over the superb U.S. Rodman Naval Station for use as a general commercial port. U.S. warships could be shut out, and Communist Chinese warships let in.

• Article 2.8 authorizes Hutchison Whampoa to "transfer contract rights" to any third party "registered" in Panama. This could be Iraq, Iran, Libya, or of course Communist China — bad news for a secure Canal.

• Article 2.10c grants Hutchison Whampoa the "right" to operate piloting services, tugs and work boats, inferring control of Canal pilots. In other words, Communist China could control the critical Canal pilots — and in turn which ships go through the Canal and when — through their ally Hutchison Whampoa.

• Article 2.10e grants Hutchison Whampoa the "right" to control Diablo Road and Gaillard Avenue as private roads instead of public roads, thereby cutting off access to strategic areas of the Canal.

• Article 2.12a grants Hutchison Whampoa priority to all piers, including private piers, at Balboa and Cristobal, plus an operating area at Albrook Air Force Station. Will the Chinese J-11 attack aircraft use this operating area in the future?

• Article 2.12i guarantees Hutchison Whampoa the "right" to designate their own Canal pilots, change the rules for boarding vessels and add additional pilots – if clients claim dissatisfaction. One client who could claim dissatisfaction is, of course, Communist China.

If it is obvious to everyone I spoke with in Panama that this major policy shift away from cooperation with the United States is the result of "money under the table" (bribes), what is the reaction of U.S. policymakers? I read one report written by an aide to a United States Senator, in which this was described as the Panamanian way of doing business, as if we were talking about a cultural thing.

American companies, bidding on the up-and-up, have been shut out of business opportunities in Panama, prompting Ambassador Hughes to send a letter of protest to Minister of Commerce Raul Gasteazoro Arango about the "unfair treatment in Panama". However, Minister Arango is the man who negotiated the lopsided Law No. 5 in the first place, so his protest fell on deaf ears.

And so Li Ka-shing managed to secure vital port facilities for Red China. Not only that, Li has provided his communist allies with the opportunity to take over military bases throughout Panama Canal zone through Law #5. With these bases, Red China is poised to shift the strategic balance between themselves and the U.S.

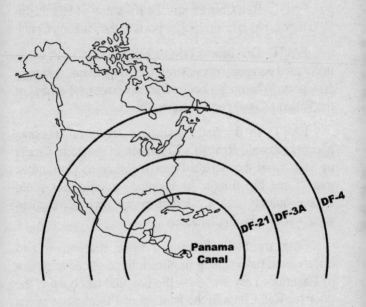

Ranges of Red Chinese nuclear missiles if they were launched from Panama.

V. THE NEXT CUBAN MISSLE CRISIS?

The subtitle of Captain Evan's first book, *The Panama Canal Treaties Swindle*, is *Consent to Disaster.* Is this subtitle becoming prophetic as the Americans move out and the Red Chinese move in?

FACT: Red China's ally, Li Ka-shing of Hutchison Whampoa, has taken over key ports at the Panama Canal.

FACT: Our recent NSC 1998 Mission to Panama uncovered company documents, including maps, revealing Hutchison Whampoa's boasts that they have total control of the Panama Canal ports of Balboa and Cristobal.

FACT: In dramatic testimony, Admiral Thomas Moorer (Ronald Reagan's Chairman of the Joint Chiefs of Staff) told the Senate Foreign Relations Committee that "I see big trouble in Panama -trouble that could evolve quickly into a conflict in our own hemisphere with world-wide implications".

"Big trouble" is right. I have researched and updated the far-reaching implications of the government of Panama's Law No. 5 — the law that has opened the door for Red China in the Isthmus of Panama and given them a foothold at our Panama Canal.

I have also consulted our Retired Military Officer's Board members and other national security experts on the implications of the Red Chinese takeover of Panama Canal installations — including Admiral Thomas Moorer, who besides being the former Chairman of the

Joint Chiefs of Staff is also the Honorary Chairman of National Security Center's Retired Military Officer's Advisory Board.

And the inevitable conclusion we have reached is that Red China has a plan for their installations in Panama. They have methodically taken over key ports and an operating area at Albrook Air Force Station. And they are poised to acquire other installations, including Rodman Naval Base.

When they are done taking over the Canal installations, Red China will use these bases to extend the reach of their army, air force, and navy — right into America's back yard. Red China will finally have a forward staging area to operate against their "number one enemy" — the United States of America.

What's worse, if Red China is planning to bring troops, ships, and aircraft into the Panama Canal bases, then they would also use these installations to correct the biggest disadvantage they have against the United States — nuclear strike capability.

Admiral Moorer has personally confirmed to me that Red China could load their intermediate- and medium-range nuclear missiles on cargo ships to any one of the Chinese ports Hutchison Whampoa runs for them. They could ship these missiles to the ports of Balboa and Cristobal that Hutchison Whampoa now controls in Panama (not to mention the operating area at Albrook Air Force Station they control and the U.S. Navy base at Rodman they have "rights" to take over). These missiles could be off-loaded in container boxes and moved right into

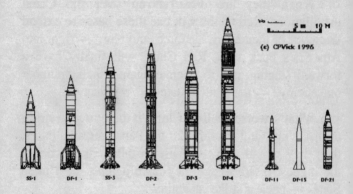

Red China's short- and intermediate-range nuclear missile arsenal. (Source: FAS Nuclear Forces Guide @ www.fas.org)

the massive warehouses at the ports. Then these missiles could be assembled and kept hidden in the warehouses, ready to be rolled out and fired on short notice.

Admiral Moorer told me what he said before the United States Senate, that "we are on what I consider to be a collision course with disaster in the very near future . . . I truly can't remember a time when I have been more concerned about the security of the country."

Like me, Admiral Moorer fears the implications of a Red Chinese takeover of the entire Panama Canal. And he fears Red Chinese nuclear missiles being deployed to Panama.

After all, there is precedent for such an action. Do you recall the Cuban Missile Crisis? In 1962 the Soviet Union brought intermediate-range missiles into Cuba, prompting a nuclear showdown with the United States.

Red China would be severely tempted to bring their intermediate-range into Panama, for several reasons, similar to the motivations of the Soviet Union in the Cuban Missile Crisis (as outlined in *Essence of Decision* by Graham T. Allison, pp. 43-56):

1. **Bargaining Barter.** Red China could use their missiles in Panama to increase their bargaining power with the United States. These missiles could be used to affect Sino-American relations regarding trade issues, the American military presence in Asia, etc.

2. **Diverting Trap.** Chinese missiles in Panama would cause great consternation in the United States. If America decided to conduct

airstrikes to destroy these missiles, it would cause an uproar in Panama and Latin America in general. Such an act would fuel anti-American sentiment in the region for years, opening an opportunity for Red China to solidify alliances — and base rights — thoughout Central and South America.

3. **Panamanian Base Defense.** Red China's hold on their bases in Panama are, at present, tenuous. The United States could bring more military power to bear in the region more quickly than Beijing. That means America could intervene militarily in Panama to take the Canal bases away from Red China. But the United States would be far less likely to send in the troops if it was known than Red Chinese nuclear missiles were there. In fact, an American invasion of bases that housed the majority of the Red Chinese intermediate-range nuclear arsenal would most likely prompt Beijing to launch those missiles, rather than lose them. These missiles would provide Red China with a serious deterrent capability to protect their bases.

4. **Sino-American Politics.** Beijing could choose to put missiles in Panama as a bold move to present the United States with a *fait accompli*. In other words, confronted with nuclear missiles in Panama, the United States would react indecisively. Diplomatic protests would only advertise the hollowness of the Monroe Doctrine and the weakness of American leadership. Such

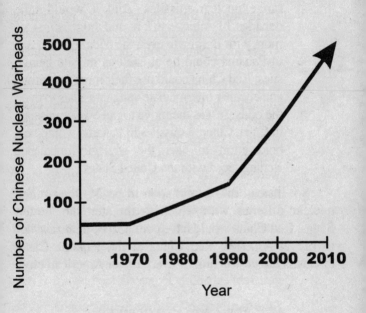

Red Chinese nuclear buildup.

weakness would alarm American allies in Asia, who depend on American security guarantee's to protect them from Red Chinese aggression. That would disrupt America's entire alliance system in Asia and the world.

5. **Missile Power.** Red China is woefully far behind the United States in number of long-range nuclear missiles. And it would take decades of intense effort and huge sums of money for Beijing to even the odds. But if bases in Panama could be utilized as missile launch sites, Red China could use their more numerous and cheaper intermediate-range missiles to even the odds. Just as the move to put Soviet missiles in Cuba, Chinese missiles in Panama would be a bold effort to alter the strategic imbalance Beijing faced with the United States.

So, instead of 18 (and soon to be 24) long-range nuclear missiles with which to threaten the United States, Red China would have over 150 nuclear missiles to fire at America. Red China at the Panama Canal threatens the destruction of every major American city!

RED CHINA'S MISSILES

Red China currently deploys only 18 (and soon to be 24) long-range nuclear missiles capable of striking the United States. The DF-5 (Dong Feng-5, also known as CSS-4) is the current model of Red Chinese ICBM deployed. The DF-5 has been compared to the old Soviet SS-18 ICBM, and came into service in 1981. In

18

Number of Red Chinese missiles that can hit the United States, 1998

148

Number of Red Chinese missiles that can hit the United States with Chinese control of Panama Canal bases

Increase in Red China's nuclear missile strike capabilitie against the United States with launch sites in Panama.

1983, the DF-5 underwent several improvements to increase its range to over 8000 miles.

New generations of Chinese long-range missiles are nearly ready to deploy. The DF-31 will be a single warhead missile with a range of 5000 miles. This missile will be silo based and have a solid fuel propulsion system. Deployment has likely already begun, and will be finished by the year 2000.

The DF-41 ICBM, due to be deployed in 2010, will have a range of over 7500 miles. More ominously, it will have an undetermined number of MIRV's (Multiple Independently-targeted Re-entry Vehicles), significantly increasing China's ability to deliver nuclear warheads.

The Red Chinese intermediate-range nuclear arsenal is formidable. The oldest such missile still in service is the DF-3, the first truly indigenous Chinese ballistic missile. The DF-3 came into service in 1971, and they were upgrading to DF-3A's in 1986. The DF-3A is about 60 feet long, has a range of over 1800 miles, and carries a single 2 megaton warhead. Their original targets were Subic Bay Naval Base and Clark Air Base, the American military installations in the Phillipines. Currently the DF-3A's are targeted at Russia.

The DF-4 came into service in 1980. Though called an ICBM, it is more accurately designated an intermediate-range missile. The DF-4 is approximately 90 feet long, has a range of nearly 3000 miles, and carries a single 2 megaton warhead. Their original target was Anderson Air Force Base, the U.S. Air Base at Guam. The DF-4 was originally deployed in silos, but later some were fitted to be deployed in caves. Those models were designed to be rolled out from their caves to their launch pads, fueled, and fired. You can imagine it wouldn't take much effort to convert these cave-based missiles to warehouse-based missiles in Panama.

The DF-21 came into service in 1988. The DF-21 is China's first solid fuel ballistic missile. It is also the first truly road mobile missile, mounted on a transporter erector launcher vehicle. The DF-21 uses a "cold launch" system, where the engines ignite while airborne. That means they can be launched with little or no notice. The DF-21 is about 30 feet long, has a range of over 1100 miles, and carried a single 200-300 kiloton warhead. The DF-21A is an improved variant with a longer range. These missiles would be ideal for deployment in the Panama ports. They are small, road mobile, and require little preparation time for launch. They could be hidden in warehouses, rolled out onto open areas of the Canal port facilities, and launched quickly.

Red China is rapidly increasing and modernizing this intermediate-range missile arsenal. The *Washington Times* (July 10, 1997) reports that "China is upgrading its medium-range missile forces with newer mobile systems." China is upgrading their old DF-3A liquid fuel missiles to new, solid fuel launchers. The Cuban Missile Crisis proved that liquid fuel launchers took too long to launch and were ineffective in a crisis. Solid fuel missiles can be launched much more quickly. These modernized missiles would be perfect for deployment in Panama. By 2002, China would likely have replaced all of its old DF-3A missiles with new solid fuel missiles which employ advanced radar guidance, making them extremely accurate.

MISSILES ARE INEVITABLE

There are those nay-sayers out there who try to proclaim that Red China would never put nuclear missiles in Panama. I have already given five reasons for such action outlined in *Essence of Decision*. But Red China's own strategic plan puts them on an inevitable path to deploying missiles in Panama.

Once Macau is taken over in 1999, the next target of Red China's territorial aggression is America's ally, Taiwan. Red China knows that Free China on Taiwan will not surrender without a fight, and that war is also a possibility with the United States if they attack.

Remember, in 1996 when Red China was "testing" missiles to intimidate Taiwan, the U.S. sent warships to the Taiwan Strait to warn Red China off. Red China responded by threatening to "rain down fire" on Los Angeles. With only 18-24 nuclear missiles that could fire at the U.S. — and thousands of American nuclear missiles that could fire back — this threat wasn't so credible.

But with over a hundred intermediate-range missiles in Panama ready to launch, the threat would be far more dire. In fact, it could be the Red Chinese plan to attack Taiwan, and at the same time announce that they have intermediate-range missiles at their bases in Panama. Red China could tell the United States not to intervene or else face nuclear destruction.

Would Americans be willing to risk nuclear war to save Free China? Would a president like Bill Clinton have the courage to go to war to stop Red China's aggression?

If this Red Chinese plan worked, it would signal the fall of the United States in the Pacific and probably as a superpower. Red China would eventually conquer Free China, and with their economic and military resources — not to mention the excellent strategic position Taiwan would give — be able to dominate the Pacific Rim for decades to come.

This scenario is rather disturbing. Disturbing for its implications, but also for its realism. All the signs point to this being Red China's plan exactly. We have thoroughly documented Red China's imperial ambitions and military build up. We know they have control of key Panama Canal ports through Hutchison Whampoa and are poised to take over other military installations. Admiral Moorer and others have confirmed that Red China can bring intermediate range nuclear missiles into the bases they already control at the Panama Canal. It is just a matter of time before we are facing the next missile crisis.

SOLUTIONS

To date, the Clinton Administration has done nothing to prevent or deal with this national security disaster:

- They have ignored our reports in 1997 that Hutchison Whampoa had a secret deal to take over the Panama Canal ports.

- They ignored shocking information about Panama's Law No. 5, which gave Hutchison Whampoa far-reaching rights to take over U.S. military installations in Panama.

- And they ignored clear evidence that Hutchison Whampoa is a proxy of Red China.

- Their CIA turned down a National Security Center Freedom of Information Act request I filed, seeking access to the documentation that reportedly shows the CIA knew all along about the Red China-Li Ka-shing connection.

- The Clinton Administration's CIA Oversight Board turned down our FOIA request claiming it was "not in the national security interests of the United States to confirm or deny" the existence of such documents.

Now that Red China has control of the key Panama Canal ports, and now that Admiral Moorer has confirmed that these ports can hide Red Chinese missiles, the United States must act to defend its interests. So what should the U.S. government do to prevent this disaster? We recommend three basic steps:

1. Proclaim that the United States will not hand over any more American military installations at the Canal to the government of Panama. As Admiral Moorer suggested in his Senate testimony, "halt the process." I suggested to friends in Panama while I was down there, the railroad car is off the tracks, continuing at full speed isn't an option.

2. Block any Red Chinese cargo ships heading to the Panama Canal which are suspected to be carrying nuclear missiles. Either we are allowed to board and inspect, or those ships should be turned away.

3. Convene emergency hearings in the United States Senate and House, to determine what political, economic, and military means should be brought to bear to ensure that Hutchison Whampoa is evicted from Panama and the United States military remains at the Canal. This should be emphasized as the highest national priority for the United States.

Options for Step 3 would include passing legislation like H.R. 2950, Congressman Duncan Hunters' U.S.-Panama Security Act. H.R. 2950 states that no American military installation can be handed over to the control of a foreign country by Panama (in other words, Red China) without severe economic sanctions being imposed on the government of Panama. The United States Senate could also abrogate the Panama Canal Treaties and announce a halt to any more transfers of American military installations, thereby insuring a continued U.S. military presence in Panama. And, of course, if necessary the United States could use the military to force the Red Chinese out of the Panama Canal and liberate the ports. Sending in the troops is always a risky option, but in this case the risk would be easily warranted by the need to protect our country's vital security interests.

VI. 1998 MISSION TO PANAMA

On June 14th, 1998 I led a National Security Center "Mission to Panama" fact-finding team to investigate the Red Chinese takeover of the Panama Canal ports from "ground zero". This was NSC's third "Mission to Panama." It lasted a full week and included visits to the Panama Canal and most of the military bases protecting it. Our team met with many important people in Panama, including government officials, labor leaders, members of the legislature, and Panama Canal workers. Some other very important people dodged us all week, as we and they read about our daily work in the Panamanian newspapers every day. What we found was that the situation at the Panama Canal was far worse than we ever feared.

MAJOR FINDING

Our major finding from NSC's "Mission to Panama" was that we confirmed that the contract the government of Panama made with Hutchison Whampoa for the ports of Balboa and Cristobal is a direct threat to American national security. Part of our team toured Balboa, Cristobal, Rodman Naval Station, and Albrook Air Force Station — all areas Red China's surrogate company already controls or has options to take over. And we can tell you without a doubt that these bases make Red China the "gatekeeper" of the Canal. Cristobal port sits astride the entrance to the Atlantic side of the Canal, right across the water from Fort Sherman (the other ports on the Atlantic are far from the opening of the Canal).

Balboa port is the only commercial port on the Pacific side, and controls the chokepoint there. Rodman Naval Station, with three separate piers which, I am told, can berth up to six warships at once, sits right across from Balboa. In fact, control of Balboa and Rodman means both sides of the Canal on the Pacific would be in Red Chinese hands. Albrook Air Force Station, which the United States handed over to Panama in October, 1997, is a massive complex capable of being converted into a modern Air Force runway. In fact, I'm told the government of Panama plans to turn the part of Albrook they kept into an international airport. What will Hutchison Whampoa do with their operating area? Our belief is that they will use it for a missile launch area.

The second major finding was confirmation that the people of Panama by an absolutely overwhelming margin, oppose the policy of their minority-elected government. The people of Panama are pro-USA, anti-Red China. The policy of Panama today, appears to be anti-USA, pro-Red China.

MONDAY, JUNE 15

Congressman Leopoldo Benedetti. Congressman Benedetti was a wonderful man and provided us with much valuable information. Captain Evans reported in his book, *Death Knell of the Panama Canal?*, that Congressman Benedetti said "Bucket loads of money are pouring in from Asian contractors." Most people we talked to in Panama think that is the reason for the Hutchison Whampoa deal. Few people believe that the government of Panama is comprised of Communists, but rather, of opportunists who care nothing for the security needs of their country, or the workers who are being thrown out of jobs. Congressman Benedetti expanded on this for us in our interview with him. He revealed that, although he had no specific proof, bribery was rampant throughout Panama's government, and he saw no reason to exclude the Hutchison Whampoa deal from being influenced by such bribery. The corrupt government of Panama was selling out America's security and Panama's prosperity for money under the table, is the common belief in Panama.

Former Congressman Alonso Fernandez. Mr. Fernandez is a former member of the Legislative Assembly and former President of the National Assembly. He co-wrote a letter to U.S. Senator Larry Craig in 1993 advocating a continued U.S. presence in Panama after 1999. Mr. Fernandez advocates the U.S. stay in Howard Air Force Base, Rodman Naval Station, Fort Sherman, Galeta Island, and Ancon Hill. He also confirmed for us the assertion by Mr. Benedetti that corruption in the government was rampant, and that such dealings most likely took place in the Hutchison Whampoa deal.

Roberto Eisenmann, Former Publisher of *La Prensa.* Mr. Eisenmann met with us to give our team his opinions on a continued U.S. presence in Panama after 1999. His point of view was clear: No continued

U.S. presence in Panama. In fact, he argued that the only way to keep Panama "pro-Yankee" was for the evacuation of the Panama Canal bases by America. He likened the U.S.-Panama relationship to a parent-child relationship, and said it was time for Panama to grow up and go out on its own. Mr. Eisenmann was also just about the only person we met with who did not care what the CIA file on Hutchison Whampoa showed about that firm's ties to Red China.

Mr. Eisenmann seemed very surprised to learn that American conservatives join him in being a little distrustful of the CIA. However, this failed to convince him that it might be in our two country's mutual best interest to at least take a look at the CIA's documentation showing how Red China controls Hutchison Whampoa.

We appreciate Mr. Eisenmann's taking the time to meet with us and his very frank exchange but he did not really answer some of the key questions of our delegation, such as, how do the people of Panama benefit by firing the workers who have maintained the canal? How does Panama benefit by walking away from its friend, the U.S.A., and cozying up to Red China? And can Panama really blame the U.S.A. if we retaliate to their new strategic deal with Red China, by cutting off any and all aid to Panama?

The only explanation I heard that makes any sense as to why all the pro-USA workers at the Panama Canal are being fired, is that the money being saved can then be siphoned off under the table; that money is certainly not evident in the economy of Panama nor the maintenance of the Panama Canal.

Fernando Eleta, President of TV Channel 4. I was told that Mr. Eleta is a very successful businessman and could see that this was true just as soon as we arrived in his office at the top of one of those towering skyscrapers that silhouette Panama City. Mr. Eleta is the President of TV Channel 4 and a very influential man in Panama. His command of English was splendid, his courtesy to us in the meeting -as well as his taking the time to meet with us, was deeply appreciated.

There was not too much we agreed on. It is simply business, the deal between Hutchison-Whampoa and his country. He is very sorry that so many Panamanian workers are losing their jobs in this transition, but feels things will work out best for Panama in the long run with the current policy. He sees no problem with Red China, and the efficiency of operations of the Canal will improve, and we have nothing to worry about. As far as bribery and money under the table, yes that does happen, but nothing can be proved. He has several university degrees from the United States and is a very well informed man, and he sees no problems now or in the future. As did many others we met with, Mr. Eleta said it is the responsibility of the United States, and not Panama, to operate and maintain the Panama Canal right now and through 1999.

So any problems that might exist, are not the responsibility of his country, but are a problem to be solved by our President and Congress. Mr. Eleta does not see Communists coming to take over (as he laughingly put it), only business being done and a transition that will work out best for his country in the long run. The only thing we agreed on was that yes, it might change his mind about Hutchison Whampoa, if our CIA file documenting the link to Red China, was put on the table for all to see. And he felt that if there is such information in the files of the CIA, it should be released in the best interest of both Panama and the U.S.A.

TUESDAY, JUNE 16

Assistant Director Augusto Zambrano, ARI. We did not meet with Mr. Nicholas Barletta, the Director of ARI (the agency dealing with areas the United States has already handed over) as scheduled. He canceled on us, we were told because he got wind of our criticism of the policy of the government of Panama. Mr. Zambrano, the Assistant Director, was very gracious in taking the time to meet with us. He said his agency was pretty much just a middleman, not really responsible for overseeing Hutchison Whampoa for example (our major areas of interest), so he could not tell us anything about that. As far as the workers being fired as the U.S.A. leaves and Panama, through his agency, takes over, he said that is not really accurate. ARI just hands off the installations to whatever company is getting it, and they, not ARI, fire the workers. But doesn't ARI have the authority to make whatever deal they want with the new company? We really did not get a straight answer. What exactly is ARI responsible for then? Things started to get a little out of hand as Mr. Bill Bright Marine moved away from the "fact briefing" originally scheduled, and ripped into Mr. Zambrano pretty strongly. I put a halt to that line of questioning, although I shared Mr. Marine's frustration. It was pretty clear we were dealing with Mr. Pontius Pilate of Panama, a man who washed his hands of everything and was responsible for nothing, and who refused to allow us to videotape our interview, and nearly stopped the meeting when Mr. Marine's "strong" questioning began.

However, Mr. Zambrano did tell me that he (proudly) helped negotiate the Panama-USA treaties. When I asked if, when they were negotiating, did his side of the table anticipate that, once they got control of the Panama Railroad, that maintenance would come to a stop, the railroad would fall apart, the workers would be out of jobs? And did this disaster give us a clue as to the future of the Panama Canal?

Mr. Zambrano finally went on record with something -he said that it was the fault of the U.S.A., not his country or his ARI, that this problem occurred. The USA stopped the railroad maintenance in the 1950's. So by the time his country took over the railroad in 1979, the railroad was already not operating. But Eugene Lewis, a railroad worker, told us that was absolutely not true. He said the railroad began to fall apart in 1979, when the Panamanian government took over the railroad from the Americans.

Guillermo Ford, Former Vice-President of Panama. Our team met with Vice President Guillermo Ford at his office in Panama City. You may remember seeing Mr. Ford on television in 1989. He was on every television news program and newspaper, and on the cover of *Time*, *Newsweek*, and other news magazines. Back in 1989, when Mr. Ford became the legitimately elected Vice President of Panama, Dictator Manuel Noriega sent his thugs to beat him up. A television camera was on scene as Mr. Ford was battered over and over by Noriega's men.

Mr. Ford's courage in the face of this brutality and his steadfast stance for democracy made him a hero in both Panama and the United States. And his courage in criticizing the current government of Panama was just as impressive. He said that, although he didn't personally have any evidence, the officials in the government were receiving money under the table for the Hutchison Whampoa deal. He was very forceful on this point. He also told us that, with the Communist Chinese in Panama, he would start sleeping with one eye open.

Congresswoman Balbina Herrera. This was one of my favorite interviews. Ms. Herrera did not beat around the bush. She is a passionate defender of her point of view, which is, to put it plainly, anti-U.S.A. I always appreciate somebody who comes right out and says what's on their mind, even if we disagree. She told me on camera that our interests are different, hers and mine -she said I represented rich business interests in the U.S., while she represented the interests of the people of Panama.

I told her about the alleged wrongdoing of our President and the Loral Corporation in helping make Red China's nuclear missiles more accurate and less likely to explode in the silos on launch (70% of which are aimed at the U.S.A.). I told her how it has been documented that a lot of money went from Loral and Red China to the

President's reelection campaign and his political party, and how they are being investigated right now. In my country, Madame Congresswoman, when our business interests betray our country and our people, we investigate them and if they are guilty, we put them in jail and we impeach the President who helped them.

What about your country Madame Congresswoman? Are your business interests and your President operating in behalf of the people of Panama when 3,800 of your people are fired from their jobs as the U.S.A. turns over installations and Panama takes them over? Where is all the money going – whose pockets is that money going into? I know what the workers think. I wanted to know what Congresswoman Herrara thought. Once again, I heard the familiar argument, that sure bribery and "under the table money" activities were going on but it could not be proved.

Congresswoman Herrara's main concern was that she did not want to ever repeat the disaster of 1989. I wasn't sure which she considered a disaster: the dictator of her country who refused to allow the democratically elected President to take office, or was it a disaster that the U.S.A. sent in troops to help restore Panama's democracy?

I was reminded by one of my Panamanian friends after this interview, that this woman is of the same political party whose members took to the streets firing bullets at American boys in uniform during Operation Just Cause. I recall that some of those bullets found their mark and some of those Americans went home in body bags.

Meeting with the Congressmen. Congressman Leopoldo Benedetti brought six fellow congressmen with him for an exchange of information. They were Mario Quiel, Lenin Suere, Lucas Zarak, Armando Guerra, Victor Mendez Fabrega, and Daniel Arias. Many of these Panamanian legislators seemed genuinely concerned about a Communist Chinese takeover of the Panama Canal, and all were interested in getting more information on the matter. Congressman Benedetti even promised to come to Washington, D.C. and meet with Senator Jesse Helms if we got him proof of the Red Chinese connection with Hutchison Whampoa. I promised them that I would get our findings and research to them as soon as possible (I am sure he will find this book very helpful). I also promised Mr. Benedetti that I would redouble my efforts to force the CIA to put this information out on the table for the Panamanian and American Congress (and both our country's people) to see for themselves. We left each Congressman with a bulging information kit.

THURSDAY, JUNE 18

Mayin Correa, Mayor of Panama City. While most of the people we met with expressed disagreement with the policy of their government towards the U.S.A. and was supportive of a continuation of U.S. bases and a U.S. presence in Panama, one person stood out head and shoulders over all the rest.

The Mayor of Panama City, Mayin Correa, gave us a most gracious welcome, very strongly asked me to give her best wishes to Captain G. Russell Evans (who she met with on one of his previous trips).

Mayin Correa felt most strongly that the future of Panama could best be served by reversing the current policy which is based upon corruption, and working closely with Panama's friend the United States (not Red China) in operating and safeguarding the Panama Canal. She was by far the most outspoken person we met.

I told Mayor Correa that most people I had spoken to said any problems in the transition are the responsibility of the United States. She strongly disagreed. She said that one person, and one person alone, is responsible for the current policy and that is, President Balladeres of Panama. He has stacked the deck, with the approval of the United States, and controls the Panama Canal Commission. He is running the show. She strongly agreed with the title of our first book, *Death Knell of the Panama Canal?* – and our premise, that if the policy of both countries towards the Canal does not change, then the Canal might not be functioning in the future.

Mayor Correa was very concerned about the U.S.A. being kicked out of Panama while Hutchison Whampoa moves in. Like most of the other Panamanian leaders we spoke with, Mayor Correa very much wants to have access to any information in the possession of the U.S. government which documents the link between Hutchison Whampoa and the government of Panama.

Richard Delgaudio and Ray Bishop meet with members of Panama's Congress to discuss crisis at the Canal.

I asked the Mayor, if 71 percent of the people of Panama want a continuation of the U.S. role in helping to operate, maintain and defend the Panama Canal, why is your President frustrating their wishes?

The Mayor said he only got elected with a third of the vote, and with nine political parties, his party might win again with just a third of the vote. The problem is that the opposition to President Balladeres is divided, so he can pretty much do as he pleases with a solid minority of support.

I later learned that the popular Mayin Corrin won her third term as Mayor of Panama City with more total votes than President Balladeres got winning the Presidency of the country. "How am I ever going to explain back in the United States, that a mayor got more votes than the country's President?" I said to our host, Ray Bishop, when I learned this? Bottom line: the biggest vote getter in Panama is pro-American bases; the second biggest vote getter, winning election with a minority of votes, is President Balladeres.)

CONFIDENTAL SOURCES

I met with individuals who worked at the Panama Canal who shared their opinions (and even his home in one case) with me freely, but who feared their positions would be jeopardized if their name were revealed. I also met with active duty military and retired military, who also shared their opinions with me freely but who also requested that I not print their names. I appreciate their sentiments. Here is my report from these confidential sources.

First of all, the most brutal findings came from these confidential sources.

For example, one American citizen told me how very, very sick and tired he is of hearing about the "Reverted" properties. Every time another military installation or base or school or facility is turned over to the Panamanian government they call it "reverted." "If the Panamanians want this property to revert then America should revert it all the way back to Columbia where it came from in the first place dammit" is what this American told me." This Yankee was tired of the insults from the Panamanian government bureaucrats who were simply lining their pockets with money from all these transactions while putting down the United States every chance they could get.

The most frightening discussion of the week took place with an active duty military officer. His views were seconded elsewhere. Once all U.S. military bases are closed and all U.S. soldiers gone from Panama, what happens if the President of the United States faces a future emergency and has to send in American troops again to secure the Panama Canal? "We will get the job done" was the quiet answer. From offshore aircraft carriers, I asked? "You need to understand," I was told, that every military target was neutralized (destroyed or seized) by American planes or troops within six hours of the kickoff of Operation Just Cause." The problem is, he said, coming from a distance offshore next time, our planes will spend more time in the air going back and forth and we will have less planes since there are no "in-country" based planes. So there will be a lot less missions flown in the first six hours. There will also be less troops that can be thrown into battle in a short time. "What does that mean," I asked, "will the mission be in danger?" "No," this military officer replied, "I believe our boys will get the job done." At what price, I asked? Silence. Will there be higher casualties? Yes, he finally replied.

So the price of losing our military bases is that, if we have to send in troops in the future, the policy of President William Jefferson Clinton today to allow the withdrawal of the U.S.A. from Panama with no loud protests, will cause more deaths of American soldiers in the future.

Operating the Panama Canal, I was told by one highly trained American, won't be easy with the Americans gone. The government of Panama doesn't care that it takes years to train some of the technicians you need to operate the complicated equipment of the Panama Canal. They have no plan to replace the Americans that they are forcing out. They have no training program. They aren't going to pay the wages you need to pay to get highly skilled workers. They have some real idiots they are bringing in who can't find their rear end in the dark with both hands. You just wait when they have full authority on December 1, 1999. I predict, this source told me, that things are going to start falling apart fast once the U.S. is gone.

A well-connected businessman who requested anonymity told me that businessmen – especially shippers who depend on the Canal - are very nervous because the government doesn't care about the long term operation of the Panama Canal, only about putting friends, relatives, cronies into paid positions and milking as much short term money out of Canal operations as possible. They don't care that they are making it more profitable for shippers to find other ways of getting their goods shipped instead of the Panama Canal. There is no predictability and no stability in businessmen's minds right now as there always was when the United States ran the show.

FRIDAY, JUNE 19

Joint Press Conference. The central event of NSC's last working day in Panama was a joint press conference I had with labor leader Ray Bishop. What follows is the press release for this joint press conference:

"Labor leader Mr. Ray Bishop and Mr. Richard Delgaudio of National Security Center in Washington, D.C. are holding a press conference this morning at 11 a.m. at the Plaza Patilla Hotel. The purpose of this press conference is to discuss their findings from this week's interviews. Mr. Bishop and Mr. Delgaudio specifically oppose: 1) The decision by the government of Panama to give the ports of Balboa and Cristobal to Hutchison Whampoa, a company with close ties to Communist China; 2) The firing of the Panamanian workers — in violation of the Panama Canal Treaties — who have kept the Canal operating and maintained, and; 3) The government policy which is pushing the Americans out of Panama and inviting the Communist Chinese in."

Ray Bishop started our joint press conference with his statement, which he spoke in Spanish (I have had it translated into English):

"I would like to thank everyone for coming here today. I invited Richard Delgaudio, the President of National Security Center in Washington, D.C., to come to Panama to take a first hand look at the situation here in Panama as the United States hands over the Panama Canal and its military installations to Panama. We have met with officials in the Panamanian government, the opposition, and the workers who run the Canal and the military bases, and I think I can say with assurance that the situation is far worse than Mr. Delgaudio ever imagined.

"The handover of the Panama Canal and its military installations is a disaster, for the security of the United States, the stability and economy of Panama, and the workers who have run and maintained the Canal.

"The contract the government of Panama made with Hutchison Whampoa, the close ally of the Chinese Communists, is a clear violation of the Panama Canal Treaties. First of all, it is a direct threat to the security of the Panama Canal. Can anyone doubt that the control of Balboa and Cristobal gives Communist China strategic control of the Panama Canal? In addition, Panamanian workers have had their rights — guaranteed by the Panama Canal Treaties — violated. They are losing their jobs, thousands of them, thanks to the government handing the ports over to Hutchison Whampoa. And the Panama Canal, which the good workers of Panama have kept running and maintained, is now falling apart.

"I am reminded by Mr. Delgaudio that, back in the United States' revolution, they had help from friends in Europe to make freedom and democracy their way of life. Panama needs such help today. So I am announcing the formation of a "Union Solidaria" movement. Together, through this "Union Solidaria" movement, I hope the people of the United States and Panama can work to keep the good jobs in Panama, keep the Communist Chinese out of Panama, and save the Panama Canal for all of us. All that I am asking from Mr. Delgaudio is that he go back to the United States and tell his fellow Americans what he has seen and heard this week. Tell them that the Panama Canal Treaties have been violated. Tell them that Hutchison Whampoa, a Communist Chinese company, has taken over the ports of the Panama Canal. Tell them that the workers of Panama are losing their jobs because of it. Tell them that the Panama Canal is going to fall apart under the control of the corrupt government of Panama. And tell them that the people of Panama need their help, and their prayers, to set them free. "Union Solidaria"."

I followed Mr. Bishop's wonderful statement at our press conference, which I spoke in English and was translated for the press into Spanish:

"Yes, Union Solidaria. Thank you very much, Mr. Bishop. You were right. This week's round the clock, night and day meetings with Panamanians at all levels of society have me convinced that there are indeed some real problems in the transition of the Panama Canal.

There are serious questions about whether the terms of the Treaties between our countries are being adhered to with the firing of 3,800 workers who have helped operate and maintain the Canal and the installations which safeguard it. It is clear that despite questions about Red China's involvement through Hutchison-Whampoa in running the strategically vital ports of Panama, Balboa and Cristobal, the government of Panama has proceeded full steam ahead.

"I could find no evidence this week, that the national security concerns of the United States nor the economic or national interests of the Panamanian people, are best served by the current policy of the current President of Panama and the current President of the United States.

"Clearly, the government of Panama is not interested in responding to our concerns or in answering any of our questions. Clearly, they are not going to help us understand why a policy opposed by 71 percent of the Panamanian people, is being implemented by the governments of the United States and of Panama. Only one person well connected in government, the gracious Mayor of Panama City, Mayin Correa, gave us a straightforward answer. And her opinions sounded most like the workers we talked to this week -the opinion that the only party benefiting from the current policy is the ruling class led by the President of Panama. Mayin Correa very strongly seconded the opinion of the overwhelming majority of Panamanians we spoke to, that she wishes to see a continuation of the U.S. role in helping operate and maintain and safeguard the Panama

Canal, and she has no wish to see Red China move in while we move out.

"And so I am honored to respond to Mr. Ray Bishop's call and the call of the workers who operate and maintain the Canal and the military bases which guard it, for the formation of a Union Solidaria movement, patterned after the one organized by that great Polish patriot and freedom fighter, Lech Walesa. In 1980, Lech Walesa bravely led a group of workers in standing up to an oppressive communist regime in Poland and their masters, the Soviet Union.

"Today, Mr. Ray Bishop and his freedom fighters remind me of Lech Walesa, as they make a stand against Red China coming to Panama, and in favor of the ideals that unite our two countries in friendship.

"In 1980, I proudly displayed my American SOLIDARITY bumper stickers and expressed my support of those freedom fighters in Poland.

"When I return to the United States, I will help organize a support coalition called UNION SOLIDARIA/Panama-U.S.A. Friendship. This Union Solidaria will express support for 1) a future of continued friendship between our two countries, (2) continuing, in partnership with Panama, the U.S. operation, maintenance and safeguarding of the Panama Canal, (3) keeping Red China out of Panama, and (4) treating Panama's workers fairly who have done such a good job of working with the U.S. for the splendid operation, maintenance and safeguarding of the Panama Canal. This is our mission statement. We urge unity (union) among people of goodwill in both countries in the hope of achieving these goals, and we in the United States express Solidarity with the people of Panama in standing up for these beliefs.

"Next month, we will be holding a major conference in the U.S. House of Representatives Rayburn Office Building for Senators, Congressmen and their staff to brief them on our findings and gather support for UNION SOLIDARIA and the ideal of Panama-U.S.A. Friendship. We will have as our honored guests at this conference, Mr. Ray Bishop and his delegation of Panamanians. Already, a number of U.S. Senators and Congressmen and their staff have agreed to meet privately and in person with Ray and his delegation to exchange ideas and information.

"Finally, I want to thank all of the people of Panama for their assistance and hospitality to us during this, our 4th Mission to Panama, especially the very gracious and popular Mayor of Panama City, Mayin Correa. The desire of Panamanians for a future of friendship and cooperation with the United States has been made very clear to me. I can see that Panamanians by overwhelming numbers, are concerned about decisions being made by government officials with overstuffed back pockets. They are concerned about the lack of maintenance of the Canal causing a future breakdown. They are worried about layouts and dismissals and lack of severance pay and broken promises -a policy which does not benefit the people, the economy or the national interests of Panama.

"I believe the people of Panama and the United States have a heritage in common when it comes to the Panama Canal. We have a future with a common interest of operating the Canal in the best interest of the people of Panama and without jeopardizing the national security interests of the people of the United States. And we have a joint interest in keeping Communist China away from the most vital maritime gateway of the world, as the Chairman of our organization's Military Officers Advisory Board, Admiral Thomas Moorer, described it.

"On my return to the United States, I will be proud to pass the word to my fellow Americans, that by overwhelming numbers, the Americans of Panama and the United States have a common interest in the future and I will encourage them to speak out for that interest. Union Solidaria."

DISAPPOINTMENTS

Several disappointments. The Foreign Minister of Panama cancelled his Friday appointment with us, presumably after reading the newspapers and seeing the kind of questions we were asking. The President of Panama could never find time in his schedule to meet with us and exchange views on the future of the Panama Canal. Our United States embassy to Panama, which was caught flat-footed by passage of Panama Law Number 5, never took the time to meet with our six-man team of U.S. taxpayers who pay their salary. Whose embassy are they anyway?

Hutchison Whampoa got repeated phone calls from Ray Bishop and his people trying for an interview. Then Winchell T. Hayward of California, one of our supporters and a Team Member, spent two days trying to arrange the appointment, only to be told by Mr. Jeffrey Bayley, deputy general manager, that they absolutely had to talk to the head of the delegation (me) before they could determine a time to meet with us. Mr. Bayley, we were told, would call me on Thursday morning. He didn't. So I called him on Thursday late morning, the next to last day of our trip. I explained very briefly that we were interested in learning more about the plans of Hutchison-Whampoa for the operation of the ports because it affected the national security interests of the United States. I objected to their delaying this matter all week, pointing out that no one we had met with all week had demanded to speak to me first by telephone, as a condition of meeting with our U.S. delegation in person. He said it was all a matter of scheduling and that he would get back to me (everywhere I went that week, Mr. Ray Bishop or I carried a cell phone for the constantly changing schedule). I never heard back from him.

Having tired of waiting for a response from Red China's agent in Panama, Hutchison-Whampoa, we changed our schedule and our tactics and split up. On Thursday, our video camera crew went to the Atlantic Ocean side (a half-day round trip) to film installations there, accompanied by Panamanian Rohelio Thirwall. Our supporters, led by Winchell T. Hayward of California, visited the nearby locks of the Panama Canal (and took some excellent photos), accompanied by Panamanian Luis Rivera.

And I undertook guerilla operations with Ray Bishop, by simply showing up at the door of "Panama Port Holdings—The Port Authority". Ray explained to the armed guard, standing in front of a doorway with a metal-barred door, that we were here to speak with someone abut the operations of the port and take pictures. I took pictures of Ray and the guard, who let us in.

On the second floor landing, I leaned out a very large (and open) window, and took pictures of the port which guards the entrance to the Panama Canal on the Pacific side. On the third floor, I took pictures of the receptionist and Ray Bishop while he explained why we were here, and how we had been trying to get this appointment all week. After awhile, we heard the guard who had let us in, get summoned up the three flights of stairs.

Apparently they did not realize that Ray spoke Spanish, because the guard got chewed out by the receptionist for letting us in (speaking in Spanish). She then explained (in English) that everyone was busy in a meeting and they would have to call us back (which they never did). I walked out carrying the "Panama Ports Company" brochure (the front company for Hutchison, which is the front company for Red China) in my hand and a batch of photos to be developed.

Two drawings from the Hutchison brochure, show very simply and clearly, why Hutchison (and thus Red China) is now the Gatekeeper of the Panama Canal. On both the Atlantic and Pacific sides of the Panama Canal, the strategically placed ports guard the entrance and exits to the Canal. There are also two large color photographs in the brochure and also on the wall in the reception room (which I photographed) illustrating the exact same point.

PANAMA'S MEDIA

The media in Panama covered our trip extensively, and we did interviews for television, radio, and newspapers. I was especially pleased by the media coverage of our meeting with Panamanian Legislator Leopoldo Benedetti on Monday, our mid-week press conference and meeting with Panamanian Congressmen on Wednesday, and our final joint press conference on Friday. Our team made front page news in the Panamanian papers.

One disappointing note I have to relate to you, however. I am told that 80% of the press in Panama is owned by the government of Panama or its cronies. And when government officials got wind of our investigation of their corruption, I was told they shut down all the media coverage of our team or had reporters misrepresent our mission. Indeed, some articles said the *exact opposite* of what we told the media. But these corrupt government officials could not cut us off entirely from the people of Panama. Several independent papers covered our "Mission to Panama", and international news organizations could not be silenced by the Panamanian government. And this book will be distributed by our friends in Panama.

EPILOGUE

For all these years, as a conservative, I've spoken and written of the kind of country we want to leave for our sons and daughters.

The importance of having a strong and capable military so that those sons (and daughters sometimes) who serve in that military can execute the orders of their Commander in Chief with confidence that when they put their lives on the line for their country, it will be for good purpose. And, good chances of success in accomplishing their mission, and good chances for their emerging with life and limb intact.

I have been dedicated to the principle of a strong U.S. military since becoming a conservative activist at age 15 so many years ago. But this stopped being an abstract principle or concept for me right about the time I was putting the finishing touches on this book.

The oldest of my three children just turned 18 and has started basic training, U.S. Army. After basic and Advanced Individual Training (AIT), he has a commitment for airborne training and a commitment (in writing) for a coveted assignment to an elite Ranger battalion (where further training will take place).

Lee and I (together with his younger brother Jason) became advanced skiers together, advanced belts in Tae Kwon Do together. Together we earned scuba diving basic certification, advanced and finally rescue diver certification from the Professional Association of Diving Instructors (PADI).

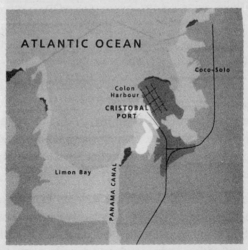

Hutchison Whampoa brags that it controls Balboa and Cristobal in its own information packets.

These activities helped show the Army that he's a serious young man. No wonder my son earned the privilege to be in the front rank of our country's national defense. Yes, I'm very proud.

But this also means that my son will be in the front rank if the war that Admiral Moorer predicted happens at the Panama Canal. So you can see that while I am proud, I am also a bit nervous right now.

So I will admit that changing the policy of the United States at the Panama Canal, is no longer just an important issue to me, but is now also a personal matter.

That interview I had back in June with a U.S. military commander in Panama, takes on new meaning to me with a son in Ranger training at this writing. That commander told me that there would be a greater loss of American lives in a future "Operation Just Cause" to secure the Panama Canal, with no U.S. military bases in Panama after 1999.

Now, today, you and I have the chance to avert that catastrophic, future loss of U.S. lives to secure the Panama Canal.

Now, today, you and I can demand an accounting of our elected officials before that fateful, last day of 1999, when the last U.S. soldier leaves and the U.S. flag is lowered from the last military base.

We urge our readers to write to your U.S. Senator and your two Congressmen. Write repeatedly seeking answers about the U.S. policy at the Panama Canal.

I pass on the pointed and astute question that Rep. Robert L. Ehrlich, Jr., asked me after we briefed him on recent developments in Panama: *"what are you doing to put this issue on the map?"* I ask your help, dear reader, to put this issue "on the map." Write letters to the editor. Call radio talk shows. Ask the magazines and newsletters you read, to cover this issue. Ask to bring me in as a speaker or as a guest on a radio talk show.

We need to keep U.S. military bases open and operational beyond the year 1999 and to continue to help operate and safeguard "the most vital maritime gateway in the world" (Admiral Thomas Moorer).

We need to remove the presence of Red China as the Gatekeeper of the Panama Canal.

At this writing, the only legislative solution in the hopper was the very well researched H.R. 2950 introduced by Congressman Duncan Hunter (whose very able staff member Bill Hawkins did splendid and original work to attack this problem). Are your Congressman and two Senators co sponsoring this bill (write to our office for a free copy of the bill)? (H.R. 2950 may be re numbered after January, 1999).

There is indeed, for the U.S.A., a *Peril in Panama.*

Only a concerted and immediate effort on the part of the citizens of Panama and of the United States to influence their elected officials will change this disastrous policy which helps neither the economy and people of Panama nor the national security interests of the United States.

National Security Center
Retired Military Officers Advisory Board

How you can help

The big book distributors told us no one's interested in the Panama Canal topic. So we self-published *Death Knell of the Panama Canal?* and thanks to our supporters and many concerned Americans we've distributed 147,000 copies of Captain G. Russell Evans' book.

With this second book, *Peril in Panama*, National Security Center is once again relying on friends and concerned Americans to help us continue this work. Captain Evans' participation in three "Missions to Panama and Richard Delgaudio's leading a fourth fact-finding Mission to Panama are all paid for by voluntary donations. NSC newsletters and other publications are paid for by individual donors.

I urge you to consider a donation to help this work continue. Consider the author of this book as a speaker or help get him on a radio or TV talk show. The year 1999 is the final year before U.S. troops are withdrawn and the last bases closed in Panama. It is urgent.

If you read about this book in a non-mainstream publication which relies upon individual donations to continue, please support them by sending them (and not us) your support. Yes, I am asking you not to send us a check, but to place your orders and your donations through that source. That will best strengthen our support network.

We urge you to make use of our publications, listed below. We've sent these to your Senators and Congressman, but their getting another copy from you, their constituent, is far more persuasive (by the way, neither Capt. Evans nor Richard Delgaudio get paid "per book sold").

Publications Available

Peril in Panama, by Richard A. Delgaudio, $6.95 suggested donation.

Death Knell of the Panama Canal? by Captain G. Russell Evans (USCG, Ret.), $4.95 suggested donation.

Big Trouble in Panama, Senate Foreign Relations Committee Testimony of Admiral Thomas Moorer (USN, Ret.), $2 (free with book order)

Red Flag Over the Panama Canal, A Report on the 1998 Mission to Panama, by Richard A. Delgaudio, $2 (free with book order)

Please add postage & handling to all orders: $2 for 1, $4 for up to 10, $10 for up to 50, $15 for 100 or more. Discount on suggested donation: 10% off on 5 or more, 20% off on 10 or more, 30% off on 50 or more, 40% off on 100 or more (a box).

Please address inquiries, orders and/or send donations to:
Richard A. Delgaudio, President ● National Security Center
P.O. Box 96571 ● Washington, DC 20090-65